The Los Angeles Times
California Home Book

The Los Angeles Times

California

Edited by
Carolyn S. Murray

Home Book

Harry N. Abrams, Inc.
Publishers, New York

Project Director: Darlene Geis
Editor: Joan E. Fisher
Designer: Judith Michael

Library of Congress Cataloging in Publication Data
Main entry under title:

The Los Angeles times California home book.

1. Interior decoration.   I. Murray, Carolyn.
II. Los Angeles times.   III. Title: California home book.
NK2110.L67   747   81-20604
ISBN 0-8109-1276-7   AACR2

Published in 1982 by Harry N. Abrams, Incorporated, New York

Printed in Japan

contents

161 the bathing experience

181 water

197 glass, light, and color

213 photographers and coordinators

The Los Angeles Times
California Home Book

introduction

The pages of this book are filled with examples of what might be called "beautiful realities." Every illustration supports the idea of real, not contrived, beauty, and contains the lesson that such beauty is the result of choices made in fulfilling one's heart's desire while meeting the practical demands of "home."

To explore this common interest in living beautifully we at HOME have joined forces with contemporary photographers and writers who specialize in home-related subjects. These professionals focus on fine art, architecture, landscape design, decorative materials, crafts, and the people who excel in creating livable environments. They record our times, documenting the way we live so that magazines, books, and newspapers, along with the audiovisual media, can pass the information along to others.

All the themes and photographs in this book have been sifted out of the thousands that were published in the pages of the Sunday *Los Angeles Times* HOME magazine. Just as the daily newspaper reports significant events and the manner in which people interact with those events, the weekly HOME edition reports on alternative styles of living. It also bears witness to the fact that if one person, in one moment of time, can create an arresting composition for living, then certainly others can follow.

The word "home" implies so many different things: connections to the past, commitments, escape, good times, solace, personal identity, a framework for the future.

The space that is home is a complex container and a living organism—it changes each day, responding to need and circumstance. Isn't it incredible that each family expects its shelter to service so many intangible concepts while still providing physical comforts and support systems for everyday activities? Yet people persist, addicted and tenacious, clinging to the idea of home, committed to keeping it theirs alone, and like a fingerprint, unique, without duplicate.

The late twentieth century is a yeasty time for the home-oriented single person as well as for the family unit. Both are definitely more concerned with the quality of life, in how they live rather than where. One consequence is that the small "forgotten" urban neighborhood has found a new generation of appreciators.

The philosophy of neighborhood has real meaning for today's families. They want to share talents and concerns, work together to plant trees, improve school systems, develop community goals. They want to take charge and be responsible for tomorrow. So they respond to the challenge of restoring an old house or pumping new life into a degenerating neighborhood. First the houses, then the shops seem to come bustling back into activity as these young entrepreneurs rediscover the inner city as a perfect place for home and business. Artists in the community often plant the seed for this revitalization. They rent lofts in abandoned factories, redesign the interiors into two-tiered habitats that combine studio and home. Always they are concerned with space rather than location.

Of course, not everyone is experimenting. People of means may still choose to live in fashionable neighborhoods, amid opulent surroundings, protected from intrusion. Even though privacy is protected, a well-maintained estate or beautiful garden can give a special lift to the passerby. Anyone may borrow ideas without embarrassment from the professionals who have contributed to the grand establishments of our time; it's part of the universal give-and-take we have achieved through mass communication. Every trip made to another city or distant country reinforces this ability to pluck ideas out of context and still make them work; the world is our museum of ideas.

As we illustrate in this book, anyone can organize a closet or a refrigerator, paint a mailbox or piece of fabric. These minor successes breed the confidence that makes major goals attainable, even for the novice. Furthermore, to take the boredom out of routine, it's amusing to develop design games around the repetitive tasks of making beds, mowing lawns, changing towels, setting tables. In the jargon of the self-improvement specialists, that is called "personal behavior modification."

In the kitchen a revolution in manufacturing has produced a generation of pushbutton, digital, computer-controlled appliances for high-speed food preparation. In the area of home entertainment, sophisticated systems are proliferating. The slickest audiovisual aids have suddenly become common adjuncts to the lives of even the youngest family members, who approach the family computer with the familiarity previously accorded a teddy bear or set of building blocks.

Interviews with members of two-income families indicate that the most desired commodity of the 1980's is freedom, translated into more free time for such special interests as art, music, travel, photography, sports, and cooking. This multiplicity of interests demands a household that can support a variety of activities, fitted with systems ready to purr into action on command, then become silent servants when the job is done.

Today's activist needs a home with inward focus, a quiet core within a protective shell. In an attempt to achieve that central serenity, many families have begun to develop small pockets of privacy. These are taking shape as garden shelters, as enclosed hot tubs, or as apartment balconies furnished with carpet, plants, and lounges. Although planned as retreats, their isolation will work only when honored by other family members.

The art of keeping things in order is appealing in every area of home living. Even collectors can attain order amid abundance. For some, the desire for perfect organization is carried out during essential daily routines, such as bathing and dressing. Unless all elements of personal care and clothing are well organized, moments reserved for grooming may be lost in frenzy instead of being accomplished in quiet luxury. Thus, the dressing room is now second only to the office in terms of order and organization.

Lately homemakers have had thrust upon them a new and challenging demand for alternative sources of energy and economical use of fuel and water. At-home conservation has become a responsibility, not an option.

For anyone ready to submit to the passion of possessing a home, the choices are there: round, square, rectangular, squat, monumental, or towering; wrapped in foliage or fringed by pools of blue-green water; on wheels or firmly planted in a sparse earth. All share a common characteristic: each is a surprise package containing a rich complexity of people, ideas, and objects. There are no carbon copies.

In spite of this diversity—or perhaps because of it—we have chosen on these pages to explore the idea of home as an easy place to be. One where there's no race to run, no prize to win . . . just the joy of sharing space, ideas, and time.

paint

Most of us merely dabble with color. We have been conditioned to prefer the pristine dazzle of white and, as a result, have almost lost touch with an intrinsic part of our visual heritage—an appreciation of the glorious gift of color.

A primitive child, born fifty thousand years before recorded time, probably enjoyed color for color's sake, and archeologists suspect that Neanderthal man daubed body and possessions with personal signatures of natural color.

Even if paint had never been invented, our lives would still be infused with color. The entire earth is a catalogue of limitless hues: a sunset is a visual explosion of oranges and reds; the sea is a mirror of tinted subtleties; a single lily stamen is so saturated with color that the russet dust is almost impossible to remove from our fingers. Experience teaches us that wild berries dye our lips and iron oxide leaves an indelible stain on stone.

Theories about the use and psychological influence of color are plentiful and amusing, if not always valid. It has been said that if we were to inhabit an all-red environment, we would soon become emotionally disturbed (red being the color of madness). In reality, the most probable disaster caused by living in an all-red space would be boredom. The eye will very soon reject the red and begin to see gray. Even an all-white interior will be perceived in shades of gray, a phenomenon caused by the tonalities of natural, artificial, and reflected light. Generally speaking, monochromatic schemes are tedious unless bold patches of other colors find their way into the palette.

Other cultures have had longer exposure to the delights of color; many have discovered the power of pure white. The way an exterior wall is painted may also affect the quality of the interior climate, since darker colors absorb heat, light ones reflect it. Every home is a potential laboratory where family members share an experiment in the way color works best.

In this chapter we present a portfolio of innovative ideas to stimulate a new round of color experiments. The focus here is on paint and pigments, for whether you are covering extensive surfaces with color or accenting a particular article or element of design, paint is the cheapest, fastest, and most effective decorating tool available.

Whether applied with fingers, brushes, rollers, pads, sponges, or jet sprayers, a rainbow of color in the guise of paint is waiting for your first timid daubs of exploration.

exteriors

There is an international language of color expressed in the painted facades shown on these pages. Sometimes the message is discreet. Sometimes it's eye-poppingly bold. Always it is appropriate and purposeful. Color can be functional when it is used to delineate such architectural elements as windows and doors. Or it can be used in broad planes to create a powerful composition that masks the underlying structural form.

Color as an important ingredient in exterior decoration began to reappear in the United States during the 1960's and '70's. Paint is a preservative as well as a restorative—wonderful for highlighting the best of Victoriana or refurbishing a facade grown drab through years of weathering. A delectable example of vintage gingerbread graces one of the streets in the turn-of-the-century resort town of Santa Cruz, California (*above*). Grand dames of Victoriana such as this have been brought back to life with inspiration, paint, and repairs. In downtown Seattle, architect Ralph Anderson helped save the historic but decaying Pioneer Building (*left*) from demolition. While the structure needed to be strengthened, its restoration mainly depended upon repair and refurbishing.

In Italy whole neighborhoods are treated to cosmetic overhaul through the delightful art of trompe l'oeil. In this cradle of the graphic arts, the work is so masterfully executed that you can barely separate the real architectural detail from the painted one. In Bogliasco, Recco, Comogli, Santa Marguerita, and Portofino local painters work ornamental miracles on rather prosaic structures such as the Giuseppe Schevone residence on Via Aurelia in Comogli (*right*).

16

exteriors: graphics

Bold graphics on boats, houses, and exterior walls proclaim the owner's individuality and make a statement in favor of contemporary design.

Houseboats needn't be exempt from the decorative art of house painting. Those who dwell on the water have already broken with tradition, so they can make an easy transition to unconventional use of color and design. This entrance to a floating residence in Portage Bay, Washington (*right and far right*), is a sophisticated domicile with abstract murals embellishing two elevations.

Muralist Arthur Mortimer puts the stamp of ownership on the outside wall of a house with this larger-than-life portrait of its occupant (*above*).

interiors: the wall as a canvas

A bare wall is always a temptation to the artist. It is a canvas awaiting paint. One can choose the subtlest interior tones or, like artist/photographer Paul Paree, wield color with bold and masterful strokes.

Paint is cheap, beautiful, and accessible, and once you begin to solve problems with it, according to Paree, it's almost impossible to stop. You keep asking yourself, "What else can I do?" Paree has answered that question many times. In his office (*right*), the answer was a straightforward geometric mural painted directly on the white wall.

For a spectacular bathroom (*below*), he conceived the painted moldings edged in gold to outline a striking graphic design on the wall behind the bathtub. Converging rainbows provide a unique and whimsical background for the toilet's utilitarian form, further evidence of Paree's bold, bright, and uninhibited approach to painting walls.

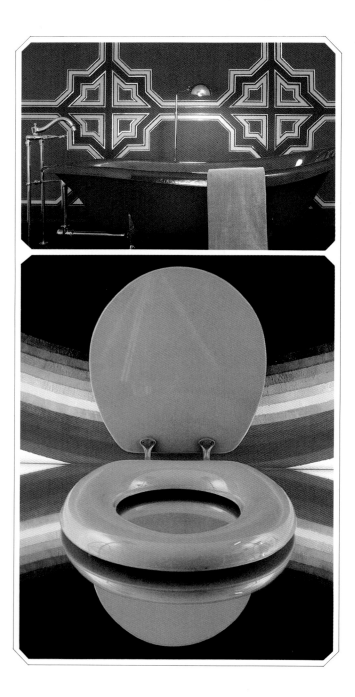

free in spirit

For the uninhibited, there's the exotic approach. Here a painterly jungle with lush tropical foliage transforms a kitchen into a work of art (*left*). Walls, cabinets, and appliances are overrun with flora and fauna that seem to be right out of a Rousseau painting. These were executed by muralist Brice Wood for a very functional kitchen designed by Suzanne Geismar.

Actress Sally Struthers settled down to sleep beneath this three-panel painting of a field of flowers that substitutes for a headboard (*right*). The idea was developed for her former apartment by designers Jay Steffy and Philip Campbell.

eye-catching devices

The eye responds when visually told where to look, where to walk. And it enjoys the surprise of visual double take—the awareness that something special is happening here.

The wall of lighted niches framed in paint (*left*) contains an unusual and varied collection of folk art from Mexico. Created by designer Alexander Girard for the home of Dr. Robert Scoren, it organizes dozens of small objects into one handsome, clutter-free composition that instantly catches the eye.

The kitchen (*right*), decorated with graphic messages, has a palette that might have been plucked from a fruit bowl. Plum, grape, lemon, orange, and lime make you think of something to eat the minute you enter.

a subtle message

Artwork, polished wood, and rug and fabric motifs all contribute to the total finesse of an interior. In an updated Pasadena townhouse restored by Phillip Lynch, paint has bridged the gap between diverse elements. The free-form painted stripe integrates walls and ceiling in this spacious living room. The color scheme was established by designers Jerry Balest and Stephen Fife.

the floor as a canvas

The ancient art of stenciling sets the stage for a revival in hand-painted "floorcoverings." All one needs is a motif that may be repeated dozens of times to form a pleasing composition. It is a refreshing way to dramatize particular areas and emphasize colors and designs.

When Los Angeles artist Lawrence Burke tackled a hall at the foot of the stairs (left), he patterned his floorscape after the floral motif of the wallpaper. Then, after sanding, staining, and finishing the fine hardwood, he stenciled and painted the design and used an acrylic resin as a final protective finish.

Muralists Lindsay Field and Matt Stevens developed a painted rug for designer David Ramey, A.S.I.D. (above). Motifs were inspired by a batik cotton fabric, and three stencils were cut out. For step-by-step instructions on how to re-create this striking stencil pattern, please turn the page.

making a stenciled area rug

There's something adventurous about the idea of stenciling a frankly fake rug onto a wood floor. Perhaps we see a wood floor as something precious and hesitate to tamper with it. Yet wood takes naturally to paint; why not chance it and apply some decorative color to the floor?

A clean surface is mandatory for stenciling. If the wood flooring has a sealed finish, a wash with turpentine will prepare the surface so that paint will adhere. Then, once the basic plan and masked area are resolved, the proper tools and paint materials will facilitate the project.

The next step is to trace some motifs, simplifying the drawings until only the basic outlines exist. Those outlines are transferred to stencil paper and then cut out. It's necessary to have one stencil for each color element in a design, therefore two stencils will be needed for the corner medallion motifs, one stencil for the border pattern.

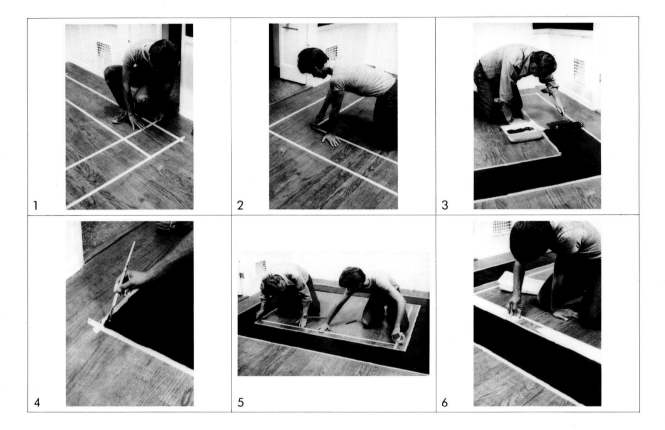

1   On a clean floor, begin by masking the area to be stenciled. A string outline might be a good first step. Then masking tape can be positioned in straight lines. Once all tapes are in position, cut away unnecessary portions.

2   To prevent paint from bleeding under tapes press out any air bubbles or gaps. A handy tool for this purpose is a brayer—it's a miniature roller. Consistent pressure with this tool helps create a perfect bond between tape and floor.

3   Once tapes are secure, cover the area between them with interior-grade vinyl paint in a flat finish. A conventional paint roller is the most practical tool for this job. The lightweight roller tray filled with paint may be kept nearby. Wipe up any spills as work progresses.

4   When the broad area of color is perfectly dry, select an artist's paintbrush and begin to touch up any missed areas with paint. Pay particular attention to corners and edges for a truly professional look. Allow drying time.

5   Begin to mask out the next area. Lindsay Field and assistant Matt Stevens worked together to create a narrower band as an accent. They repeat the masking technique and pressure with brayer, as described in Steps 1 and 2.

6   To fill this narrow band of space, Field suggests a painting pad as a good alternative to a small roller. After this band is filled with color, touch up any missed areas, using an artist's brush. Allow to dry before tackling the first stencil.

STENCILING MATERIALS

stencil paper or flexible acrylic sheets
X-acto knife
stencil brush
artist's sable brush for detail work
masking tapes of various widths
brayer (available at hobby or paint stores)

paint rollers and tray
painting pads of various sizes
paper plates and cotton-tipped swabs
paint: flat-finish interior vinyl
sealer: satin-finish urethane
solvent and urethane thinner for clean up

7   To begin a corner motif, place the basic flower medallion into position. Secure with masking tape. Pour a small portion of paint onto a paper plate. Dab stencil brush into paint, then dab paint through stencil cutouts. Don't use brushing motion as it will cause smearing.

8   To avoid smearing paint, stencil must be carefully lifted. Allow medallion to dry. Note the four white dots. These are artist's register marks. When more than one stencil is used, each should have matching tiny holes that are precisely aligned.

9   While waiting for corner medallions to dry, Field begins to paint the motif that is to fill the long runs of the border. Stencils may be secured with masking tape, but an extra pair of hands is usually a better way to speed up this process.

10   When border motifs are dry, the second flower stencil may be positioned on corner medallions, with register marks aligned. Fill in color areas with stencil brush. Lift carefully. Touch up missed areas with artist's brush.

11   When motif is totally dry, details around the flower may be added freehand. Cotton swabs are convenient for this work. Field believes these freehand touches add a special "living" quality to stenciling. Experiment to create a variety of decorative embellishments.

12   Finally, review the overall design. If any major gaps exist between corner and border motifs, try working one-half of a stencil motif into the space, as shown. When paint is dry, tapes may be removed. The last step is a sealer coat of satin-finish urethane.

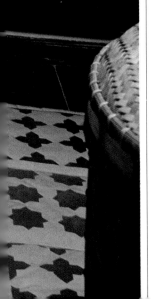

stencils: walls and countertops

Stencil motifs may be found everywhere—in the grillwork of the Alhambra in Spain, through a microscope lens, or in the garden.

Any novice can quickly become a slick stenciler, according to designer Judith B. McCormick, A.S.I.D. It all depends on the degree of patience and commitment. In creating a seating area (*left*), McCormick translated Moorish motifs from the Alhambra onto the wall, throw rug, and pillows, and even onto paper as framed art.

Artist Brooke Pattengill's white kitchen counters were painted professionally, but the idea of stenciling Formica counters and backsplash was hers (*above*). She traced the pattern for the stencil from Mexican ceramic tiles, used a blue acrylic paint sealed with two coats of Varathane, and achieved a highly decorative result for a minimal cost. Besides, the project was fun.

furniture: unfinished

For the family with more time than money here are three amusing paint projects that can be executed over a long weekend. Each begins with unfinished furniture. This trio of projects created by Ruth and Brian McKinney utilizes simple, unpainted wooden furniture. There's a rocking settee, a modular system of storage components, and a three-panel folding screen. Using stencils and freehand work, anyone could emulate—or even improve—these ideas.

The flying horse motif on the screen was easily scaled up from ordinary drawing paper, thanks to the grid system suggested by the McKinneys.

Masking tape is the secret ingredient for the children's storage system. It keeps the bands of painted color from bleeding. And by carrying the striped design through to the back wall of open storage units, the V-shaped pattern emerges more clearly.

For more about how to do these three projects, turn the page.

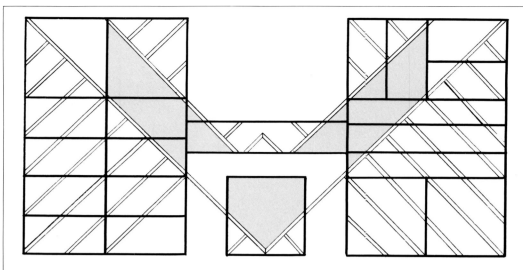

painting a child's storage wall

Masking tape is a key ingredient for this furniture project. Be sure to have it on hand before reaching the paint stage.

First, prepare unfinished units using plastic wood-fill in light wood tone as described in the rocker project. Let dry, rough sand. Apply latex undercoat to seal all surfaces. Let dry, rough sand.

Apply latex enamel in chosen background color. Let dry. Repeat with second coat if needed.

Arrange units as you plan to use them. Position units on floor, fronts up. Using ¾-inch masking tape, create stripes as indicated in drawing (*above*), beginning with the big V-shape. When tape reaches doorless cupboards, attach it to the inside back wall of each unit, so the design will be continuous. Protect adjacent areas with masking tape if wished. Finally, using high-gloss enamel, fill in areas between tapes. Note: Any section of the drawing may be used for a smaller component system or as a graphic design for wall or ceiling.

painting a folding screen

Prepare surface as described in the rocker project. Apply latex undercoat, let dry, sand. Next translate a design idea to the screen by creating a modular grill with soft lead pencil. If each panel is 16 inches wide, make square 8 inches wide (allow for frame).

Draw an outline as indicated. If decorating both sides of screen, the same outline can be reversed. Begin to fill in with oil-based enamel where needed, always allowing paint to dry sufficiently. Frame may be painted a contrasting color.

painting a rocking settee

To prepare an unfinished surface, use plastic wood-fill in a light wood tone. Apply with fingers into any unwanted gaps, scratches, or holes. Let dry, then rough sand. Next apply, as sealer, a white latex undercoat and let dry. Repeat rough sanding. Plan decoration and color scheme. Make stencils or cutout patterns for such details as tiger tails and palm-tree tops, trace outlines of these details onto settee with a soft lead pencil.

Using high-gloss enamel paints, fill in the major area of color, leaving palm fronds and tiger tails unpainted.

Using a 1½-inch flat bristle brush paint the blue sky area. The sun may be painted freehand, blending colors from orange to yellow. Fill in palm fronds and tiger tails and repeat with another coat if color values are too weak.

MATERIALS: SETTEE AND STORAGE UNIT

soft lead pencils
¾-inch masking tape
light tone plastic wood-fill
rough-grade sandpaper
1½-inch bristle paint brush
pointed, camel-hair detail brush
latex undercoat
high-gloss enamels

making a tailless-tiger pillow

Draw two simple patterns on tracing paper; one front panel, one back panel. Trace outline onto chino cloth, using black oil-based Pentel. Then fill in the details as shown.

Using Ink-O-Dye, fill in areas with color. Place fabric in direct sunlight until Ink-O-Dye colors develop. When ready, cut out tiger shapes, allowing ⅝ inch for seams.

Place painted surfaces face to face and stitch seams, leaving six inches open. Turn painted sides out, stuff with fiberfill, hand stitch to close. To make the second tiger, which faces in the opposite direction, merely flop drawings and trace.

Ruth's pillows are 16 inches when finished. She adds extra quilting details at ears, face, and hip for added dimension.

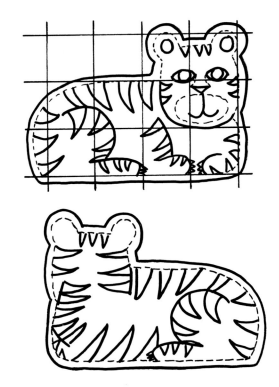

MATERIALS: TAILLESS-TIGER PILLOW

tracing paper
soft lead pencils
chino cloth
washable black marker (Pentel)
fabric paints (Ink-O-Dye)
fiberfill

furniture: finished

Illusion is a trick all artists use. By painting ribbons of color onto these stark white cubes, photographer and graphic artist Paul Paree piles illusion upon illusion. Where does one cube begin, another end? And is that a table or a wall painting?

Paree explains his approach: "Here is a cube seen through new eyes. I approach the cube from the corner, sharp and angular. Now it is a white box surrounded by a hexagon of color. It becomes a piece of sculpture, a painting you can sit on. Painted in matched pairs, the cubes can be composed and recomposed in seemingly endless patterns."

This setting (*right*) is an example of the way effective use of paint creates an environment. Four cubes—which Paree calls Supercubes—and one wall-hung card table provide total decorative impact. Remove those daring bands of color and there's nothing but an arrangement of loosely related objects.

The hanging game table solved two practical problems: how to fill wall space attractively and where to store an extra table in a rather small apartment. Paree's rainbow-framed checkerboard was an answer. Using a secondhand folding bridge table, he painted the surface, attached a drawer in back to hold checkers, designed a green-felt cover for card games, then finally hung it right on that wall!

tabletops and chairs

Take a theme and run with it. In these settings, designed by artist-photographer Paul Paree, small-scale motifs from popular tableware set a plan in motion. The designers at Anne Klein provided a wealth of artistic inspiration. On a tabletop *(lower left)*, a quatrefoil border motif from a Klein napkin has been enlarged, traced onto paper, and stenciled four times to cover the surface.

The bold colorings and Art Deco pattern of Rosenthal china have been expanded to make an original tabletop *(upper left)*. Bowknotted napkins are a "why not?" touch anyone can try.

Black lacquer has been spray-painted on all parts of these inexpensive yet classic bentwood chairs *(right)*. The seats have been decorated in a simple design with high-gloss paints, then finished with two coats of acrylic spray.

fabrics: hand painted

Minimal skills, bold strokes of color, and an original concept—that's all
it takes to produce an impressionistic wall graphic or a bold banner.
Skip realism—it will bog you down in detail. Stay loose and allow
imperfections, even paint drips, to become an integral part of the
scheme.

   White cotton duck and water-based textile paints were the ingredients
used by Ruth and Brian McKinney to develop the Field Flower hanging
(*above*). Four quickie stencils (two for buds, two for blossoms) were cut
from heavyweight acetate. Freehand stems complete the design. A stiff
bristle brush dipped in paint was worked against the stencil to develop
outlines. Short strokes were brushed toward center to create the petals.

fabrics: stenciled

Multicolored impressions pile one upon the other in this delightful print (*left*). By filling several plastic spray bottles from his palette of colors, Brian McKinney created a firmament by stenciling on a chino-cloth panel.

Fabric paints were watered down to pastel hues, then pump sprayed. Here again casual paint drips add character, like distant stars peppering a desert sky. Just a word of warning: be sure to allow each color to dry before applying another. Once dry, motifs can be overlapped without danger of smearing.

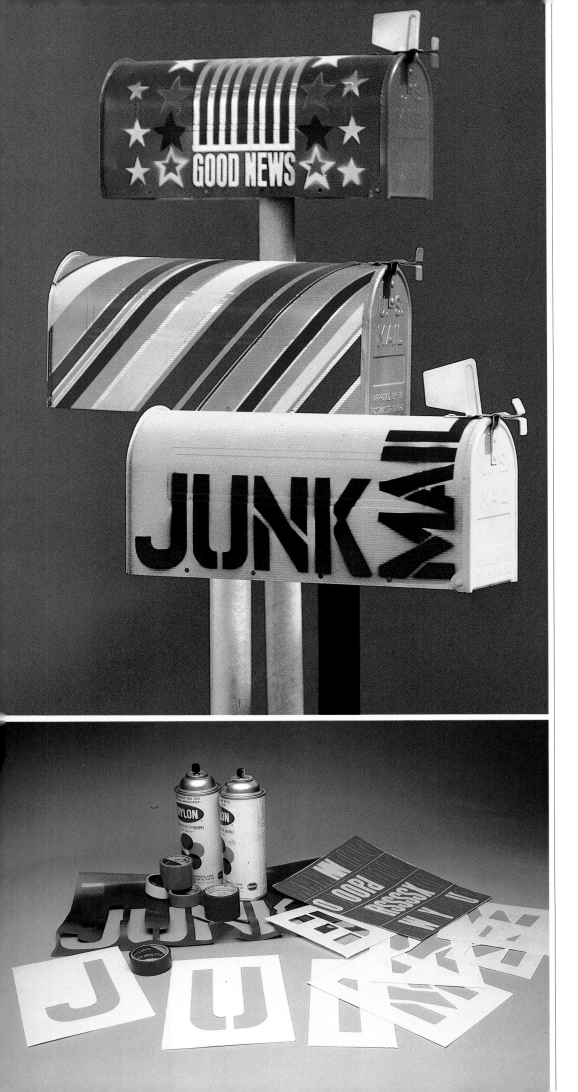

odds and ends

Special delivery for do-it-yourselfers—here is a series of cheery mailboxes and painted wicker containers for the home (*left*). Even the mail carrier deserves a change of pace. Not much is needed to upgrade a mailbox: a coat of enamel spray paint, vinyl stick-on letters, colored adhesive-backed tapes, and sheet acetate for hand-cut stencils. Design consultants Ruth and Brian McKinney made this trio sparkle.

Artist Barbara Golden gave these unpainted wicker accessories (*right*) the flick of her paintbrush and spiced up the bathroom. By working bath-towel colors vertically on the hamper and horizontally on the wastebasket she keeps the project from getting too matched up. Barbara uses acrylic paint, then spray finishes with clear lacquer.

children's project: fortress

No matter where they live, children like to build their own scaled-down shelters. This fortress is based on a stack of two-foot-square panels of foam core, composed and painted by the kids.

Sheets of foam core, trays of primary paint, some rollers, masking tape, scissors, plus a handful of enthusiastic youngsters got this project off the ground. Planned by designer Dawn Navarro, who says she was inspired by Charles Eames's famous House of Cards, the two-foot-square panels lock neatly into position to become an instant fortress. When day wanes, all is easily disassembled and toted back indoors.

building a children's fortress

Designer Dawn Navarro suggests that this project become a do-it-yourself venture for the children, with adult supervision.

First stop:
A building supply center. Here you'll find nearly all the materials—white bond paper, X-acto knife, latex wall paint, roller brushes, paint trays, white glue, and drop cloths. Next, visit an art and drafting supply store to get the 4 by 8-foot sheets of foam core (Navarro used three sheets). Once home, spread the drop cloth over the work surfaces and proceed as follows.

Preparing the foam core:
Measure and mark each 4 by 8-foot sheet in half lengthwise, then score at 2-foot intervals across the width. With guidance from an adult, children ten and over can cut the foam core with an X-acto knife.

Applying the paint:
All panels could receive solid color on one side; panels that end up as mistakes could be painted solid on both sides. These can be used for visual relief or as window cutouts.

Give the older children a lesson in graphics by having them apply masking tape in stripes, squares, rectangles, or combinations of these basic shapes. Next step: fill in with bright background colors.

When the paint dries, carefully remove tape, then apply new tape over the background, butting the edges of the designs. Paint these unfinished areas and let dry. Remove tape.

Cutting slots and windows:
Draw cutting lines for slots 3 inches from sides, ¼ inch wide by 3 inches deep, as shown in illustration. Cut out window shapes with an X-acto knife.

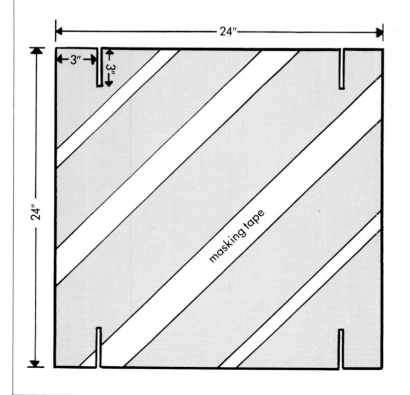

24"

3"

3"

24"

masking tape

family projects: eggs, stamps

Just about everyone likes personalized possessions: monogrammed towels, shirts, napkins, special license plates, and writing papers. Children, especially, like their own property clearly identified. Some things are decorated for the moment and quickly destroyed— gift wraps, eggshells, etc. Even so, each is an exercise in design and self-expression.

Eggs offer the promise of new life, the gift of nourishment, and the pleasure of observing how form follows function. But there's always the awareness of impending disaster—the momentary shock of discovering the frailty of one of nature's engineering marvels. While we have them, we like to leave our mark on their pristine surfaces. Decorated hard-cooked eggs can't be expected to last more than a few months without spoiling. And if decorated eggs are to be eaten, only FDA-approved food colorings and dyes may be used.

Artist Catherine Cartwright Jones paints a miniature cityscape, against a sky-blue background (*left*).

There's almost instant success in creating a pattern with giant rubber stamps (*above right*). The same motifs can be used to create place mats, nametags, lunchbags, gift wraps, ribbons, and notepaper. And stamp pads may be inked in a variety of colors, allowing the imagination to run free.

Youngsters can make their own stamps by pressing the eraser material over a heavily penciled design, then cutting away the negative part of the motif. Or they can carve letters or designs from inexpensive plastic or rubber erasers. Using a soft lead pencil, make a drawing on a piece of paper. Place face-down on eraser and press. Drawing will transfer to eraser. With an X-acto knife (#11 blade) cut away uncolored areas, leaving raised design. Let children experiment . . . it's an inexpensive game.

53

children's project: clowns

After everything else in your environment has been painted, one thing remains—you. As a final colorful project why not follow the suggestion of the song *Be A Clown?* Somewhere deep inside each of us lies the makings of a clown. The character we present to the world has a more liberated counterpart ready to burst forth with joyous, funny, even silly routines. But what's the secret to letting this alter ego loose? The greasepaint mask. It hides the old you and encourages the secret you to flower.

No two are ever alike—that's part of the tradition of clowning. The application of a funny face can bring forth that inner character full of laughter. Suddenly a zany walk, skip, or other exaggerated gesture shapes a special personality. Without a doubt, you will surprise many a little friend with the new personality that emerges, but the biggest surprise will come in watching the clown appear in yourself.

Anyone can transform his safe and sane image. All it takes is a gathering of young friends, clown makeup, and an impromptu assemblage of crazy-mixed-up clothes.

Graphic artist Dawn Navarro of Malibu, California, created this trio of characters: Star, Daisy, and Twinkle. She believes that costuming is half the fun. There is an array of possibilities—gloves, oversize tennis shoes, bib overalls, and floppy bow ties. Wigs, hats, handmade costumes, roller skates, and lifelike hand puppets add dimension. And all kinds of bells, music, and noisemakers call attention to the goings on.

Creating a clown mask is the other half of the fun. And once started the new personage is likely to find it difficult to limit the character to one theme.

entertaining

Entertaining at home is a complex activity that must appear effortless. There should be moments of fun and refreshing laughter as well as opportunities for quiet conversation. Though a house should look its best for the event, entertaining need not mean burning a hundred candles or filling a table with every piece of china and crystal in the cupboard. There's a subtle balance between the special effort and the comfortably familiar. Once it is discovered, excessive decorating and artificial moodmaking devices can be discarded for a warm and relaxed background where family and friends gather.

Perhaps there's a flaw in our semantics. Almost no one actually "entertains" at home. We feed a group of people and provide liquid refreshment, but in truth we expect guests to entertain themselves. At best we can provide bodily comforts, reasonably pretty table settings, and physical space in which to eat, drink, and make merry.

The ideal partygiver is never a fanatic about the food and its consumption. Good and unusual dishes are presented for the guests' pleasure rather than as an ego trip for the hosts. Nor should the drinking of wine be treated as an esoteric experience, unless all gathered are wine devotees. Perhaps the last indication of the occasion's success is revealed in the way guests wind up the evening. If they leave lighthearted, high spirited, and laughing, it's a good sign that the host is on the right wavelength. If the party giver also had a good time, that is the ultimate accolade.

The real test of a great host or hostess is the pre-party organization. Anyone can "throw something together" on the spur of the moment if homework has been done well before party time. The house and everything in it become part of a personal entertainment package. Large-screen television and sophisticated sound systems have become an integral part of today's life-style. Why shouldn't these possessions be given higher priority in the overall approach to entertaining at home? The jumbo screen lends itself to exciting election-night parties, Saturday afternoon football get-togethers, and movie previews.

There is nothing more delightful than chamber music played at home by friends for friends, with refreshments afterward. Other special interests such as wine appreciation and art collecting are more fun when shared. A home art gallery or miniature wine-storage library can make a stimulating and unusual setting for parties or small gatherings. Guests appreciate having conversation starters—it takes some of the pressure off those first few moments of mingling with strangers.

Inexpensive accessories, such as plastic tableware and mass-produced goblets, may be mixed with classic forms to create a striking setting, as illustrated in this Art Deco composition by J.P. Matthieu.

formal beauty

Great hosts and hostesses realize they need a whole wardrobe of accoutrements for their tables. And they select tableware as astutely as they choose dinner partners.

Believing that each table setting can be a personal work of art, Ruth and Fred Meyer of Beverly Hills make every meal a highly satisfactory visual experience. "Food is only half the pleasure of a get-together. Exchanging pleasantries, seeing beautiful objects . . . these make the meal nourishing to the spirit as well as to the body," Ruth Meyer explains. "You wouldn't wear the same dress to breakfast that you would to a formal dinner. So why not collect a complete wardrobe for the table, including glassware, china, and flatware for every mood and occasion? Use accessories as you would jewelry . . . for a sparkling accent." Whether the possessions are of heirloom quality, as shown, or well-designed mass merchandise, the goal is to personalize your table.

Gleaming crystal stemware, candlesticks, and individual accessories from the Meyers' collection include pieces by Baccarat, Val St. Lambert, St. Louis, and Lalique. The sterling silver flatware is Buccelli Grand Imperial.

simplified settings

The new wave of freedom from elaborate culinary tradition we now find in *nouvelle cuisine* also has left its mark on the time-honored dictates of traditional table setting. But in spite of the new simplification, one important guideline remains: scale. Objects on a table need to be in pleasing proportion to one another. In this setting (*left*) glass and pewterlike plates alternate in layers that gleam in the candlelight. A service plate of pressed glass supports the Armetale dishes and chunky, stemmed glass bowls. The golden glow of fresh mimosa complements cool silver and glass forms.

Boldly eclectic, this table setting (*right*) by designer David Carlson makes the most of polished surfaces—lacquer, porcelain, silver, glass, mirror, and leather. It is a synthesis of pieces picked up all over the world and illustrates how well-traveled people like to entertain. That penchant for gathering ideas wherever we go often results in an excitingly original potpourri.

inspiration from nature

The naturalist's field book inspires both designers and consumers . . .
so things botanic have long found favor on our tables.

There's a sculptural quality to Italian designer Marella Agnelli's
composition (*left*). She has used a series of five graduated circles of
coordinated tableware, then as a change of pace, tucks in fan-shaped
butter plates. Conical, stemmed, crystal goblets, and gold-bordered
flatware add a Midas touch. An easy bouquet of exotic lilies recapitulates
the stylized floral theme of the china. And all objects float serenely on a
bare glass tabletop.

A menu featuring game birds inspired this table setting (*right*).
A tartan cloth is the background for antique pewter accessories, mugs,
Armetale service plates, and ironstone dinner plates. Stag-handled
knives enhance the hunt theme.

informal settings

Casual comfort implies a slackening of rules; it encourages unwinding. That same comfort can be achieved at mealtime, with casual style. Toting one's own tray is a wonderfully easy party solution, and it gives guests an opportunity to mingle. In this portable setting (*left*) , chilled soup and sandwiches are the menu.

There's little doubt about the scenario when Grace and Harold Robbins give a party (*above right*). The theme is established by the occasion at hand. If a friend is taking off for the Orient, Grace Robbins might set a Chinese parasol in each corner of the dining room, then place calligraphic screens as a backdrop. The see-through glass tabletop shows off round bamboo place trays set with blue and white porcelain and chopsticks. The Far Eastern mood continues with the Marbella bamboo furnishings by Kreiss.

An oversized bait basket found at Hong Kong's Aberdeen Bay supports the round glass tabletop with its tray-lunch setting (*right*). Woven textures play against smooth white porcelains when executive Robert Kreiss puts it all together for casual entertaining.

country settings

Sometimes we have to make changes to establish a home's personality. That's what the John Halls did when they remodeled a 1930's house, achieving a combination of function and charm for their countrified kitchen/dining area (*above*).

By gutting and rethinking both kitchen and dining room, the Halls were able to provide the touch of country élan they wanted as background for gourmet meals for friends and family. Hand-cut parquet floors have replaced vintage vinyl. New wooden beams and higher ceilings made it possible to install a ten-foot-tall brick fireplace. The generously proportioned table is a seventeenth-century Jacobean design; the classic Windsor chairs are nineteenth-century yew wood. The Halls used an easy mix of pewter, brass, china, and glass when setting the table, then accented them with flowers fresh from the garden.

Just about anyone over the age of reason can set a table: knives and spoons to the right, forks and napkins to the left, plate in the middle. But the design potential of the components is so varied that one should constantly question and evaluate the old patterns. To avoid the deadly dull routine of party planning, designer John Patton likes to serve a Sunday soup supper in a nontraditional locale (*right*). A blue-skied environment banded in decorative tiles provides a private niche in his kitchen/dining area. It works as well for brunch or lunch. The bread box with its bouquet of cooking utensils is removed before food is served, having made its statement by introducing a bit of whimsy.

color as the key

Color can be its own reward; when all other ideas fail, one powerful color will often establish a special party ambience.

Pick the color to suit the mood: cool blues, garden greens, sunshine yellows, or icy whites. Find shops that feature tableware from other cultures. In this all-blue setting (*left*), quilted calico place mats support service plates and fish-shaped accessories from Japan. Like objects at the bottom of the sea, the wood, lacquer, stainless steel, and crystal forms meld in the kinship of an underwater world.

Brilliantly colored wrapping paper by Faroy replaces an ordinary tablecloth with a field of irises in this composition (*right*). The garden-fresh colors are repeated in the Metlox lime-green plate and enamel spatterware casserole and buffet plate from Mexico. A fleck of golden sun is supplied by the flatware.

creative place mats

A creative dimension and a personal touch can be added to each family's wardrobe of tableware through the painting of original place mats and napkins. Here artist Ruth McKinney shows how she chose a popular china pattern (you may select your own) as the inspiration for two sets of hand-painted place mats. McKinney selected the Mikasa plate because it delivered an instant color scheme and basic concept for fabric painting. By designing two motifs—one geometric, one floral—she is able to use one as a place mat, the other as a napkin. Using white chino cloth, permanent-color dyes, and oil-based felt-tipped pens, she produced a series of delightful accessories. Her instructions and sketches follow.

making place mats

Here are Ruth McKinney's directions and materials list for four handpainted floral or geometric fabric place mats. Repeat the process for each piece desired.

MATERIALS
tracing paper
butcher paper
black and colored oil-based markers
DEKA-Permanentcolours
small bristle brushes
1 yard (45 inches wide) chino cloth
1 yard (45 inches wide) ciré or lightweight parachute-type fabric
1 yard (45 inches wide) iron-on interfacing
6 yards double-fold bias tape (for curved mats)

1   On tracing paper draw a 1-inch-square graph. Using this and the black marker, trace the desired plate design or the geometric design shown.

2   To enlarge the design, make a 2-inch-square graph on butcher paper; transfer the design square by square, making black outlines.

3   Mark the outline of the desired place-mat shape on chino cloth. Place chino cloth over the portion of the enlarged design you wish to reproduce.

4   With markers of appropriate colors, trace the design onto the fabric.

5   Paint with matching DEKA-Permanentcolours.

6   Iron the back of the fabric or place it in a warm dryer for 20 minutes to set the colors.

7   Trim excess fabric from the place mat.

8   For backing, cut corresponding ciré and interfacing. Iron interfacing to wrong side of ciré, then stitch to place mat, wrong sides together.

9   To secure edges of a curved place mat, encase outer edges with double-fold bias tape.

10   For a rectangular mat, turn edges under ¼ inch and press all sides. To finish hem, turn under another ⅜ inch, then topstitch ¼ inch from the edge on all sides.

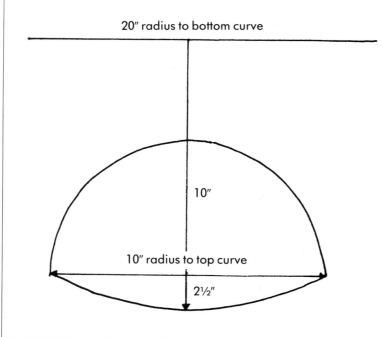

20″ radius to bottom curve

10″

10″ radius to top curve

2½″

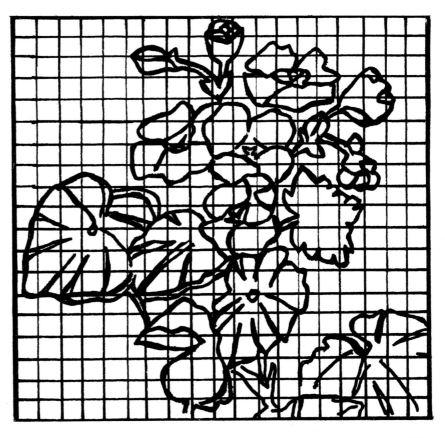

the buffet party

The buffet party, more than any other, requires a masterful approach. According to award-winning designer Rudi Gernreich, buffet settings are great exercises in design. "Each table is a still life composition; it needs balance, color, form, and it also has to function. It must be organized for ease of access and must be positioned so that party traffic will flow without bottlenecks." Here Gernreich creates a buffet-party setting that is a dramatic work of art.

Basic black and white . . . that's a formula Gernreich feels is most comfortable to live with. "Black is neutral. It never interferes with other forms, never clashes." Underscoring this design philosophy he suggests this sophisticated Chiaroscuro Supper menu and sets up the buffet on a glass-topped table. Using his limited-edition dinnerware by pop artist Roy Lichtenstein, he adds a procession of ivory elephants, black-and-white bread, black caviar, white eggs, black olives, licorice, and a snowy tureen of chilled vichyssoise. Peggy Moffitt, Gernreich's signature mannequin, added white tulips and cherry-red tomatoes, and holds a glass of almost-black Guinness stout. The result? A visually exciting collage of shapes, textures, tastes, and surfaces, all bound by one dominant color theme.

CHIAROSCURO SUPPER FOR EIGHT	
caviar	
chopped eggs	chopped onions
chilled vichyssoise	
pearl onions	whole new potatoes
italian plum tomatoes	
black and white bread	
vermont cheddar	ribier grapes
english crackers	
sugared almonds, mints, licorice, confections	
guinness stout	iced dutch gin
espresso coffee en demitasse	amaretto

parties alfresco

Whether you're poolside playing, decking it, or patio partying, it's possible to develop a do-it-with-ease approach that emphasizes mobility, practicality, and versatility. Anything goes—paper, linen, china, plastic, alone or in combination—as long as it's done with a dash of panache.

If twenty invited guests arrive as instructed, it should be easy for each to join a group, take a seat, settle down. For one amusing yet practical grouping (*above*), slatted park benches can seat four to eight (or more, if they're intimate friends), and a pair of backless benches pushed together can form the table in a cozy patio corner.

When the clan gathers around a pool, keep the food and refreshments rolling on a Lucite cart fitted with a salad bar and other service accessories (*right*).

party pull-ups

Chairs, chairs, chairs. Designers have yet to conceive the ultimate chair—there's always one more on the horizon. All the chairs shown here have been formed from pliable grasses: reed, rattan, cane . . . even rattan shavings have been utilized. Fine craftsmanship, clean design, and neutral, unadorned finishes make them favorite casual furnishings. These chairs can live anywhere, dressed up or unembellished. Lightweight and graceful, they are the greatest tool any partygiver has. Especially when it's time to say "pull up a chair."

special interests: wine cellars

The emergence of wine as a collectible has created the need for a whole new keeping room—the home wine cellar. Some are elaborately designed, following the idea of a library where one goes to study fine wines—and imbibe—on the spot.

Vaulted ceilings, old brick flooring, and handcarved beams give an illusion of a faraway place in a long-ago world *(left)*. In reality, this unusual bar and wine cellar with its murals and stained-glass accents is a modern treasure cave for a private stock of wine.

One air-conditioned wine cellar *(above)* is really a full-time dining room where wines from all over the world rest within arm's reach of the host. Designed by Frank Austin, A.S.I.D., for Freddie Fields, this dual-purpose space is just a flight of stairs down from Fields' private projection room. For all its sybaritic overtones, the cellar has a slightly monastic air, with high-backed embossed leather chairs, refectory table, flagstone floors, and rough plaster-and-straw walls.

family interests

Don't overlook the family's need for entertaining moments. Often we neglect to arrange a quiet, comfortable spot for reading or televiewing. A few peaceful hours can make an evening at home better than any party. Watch for a whole new category of furnishings designed to make those private hours even more enjoyable.

The family fans will cheer no matter what their team affiliation,

especially when they're supported by the Thayer Coggin seating—and eating—system (*left*). One of many new concepts that provide upholstered table surfaces along with cushiony comfort, these units represent a new movement toward planning for family individuality.

Stadium Seating is what it's called (*above*). It has enabled families to broaden their horizons in terms of how and where spaces may be planned for activities. Don't look now, but someone may be pulling that component out from under your handy gooseneck lamp! Designed by Milo Baughman for Thayer Coggin, Stadium Seating explodes the myth that furniture must be kept close to the wall. With these units the whole room is for sitting, reading, TV watching, game playing, eating, and enjoying.

expanded kitchens

There's a certain inviting warmth that emanates from a kitchen fitted with cozy, comfortable nooks for guests and family.

Any kitchen can be used as a stage since there are numerous bits of theatricality involved in the production of a meal. Many guests enjoy a front-row seat. A two-level island *(left)* provides an intimate proximity between chef and audience in a spacious kitchen, designed by Rosemary Yoder, A.S.I.D., and student designers Jim Rice and Karla Champion for the Showcase of Interior Design in Pasadena. The space works beautifully for Sunday brunches or informal lunches, thanks to its pleasing blue color scheme and fanciful stained-glass window.

Another combination works well in an expanded kitchen *(right)*, designed by Joan Neville, A.S.I.D. Neville was able to personalize a condominium apartment by making choices *before* her new space was finished, an option that prospective condominium owners should keep in mind. The idea is to request variations before construction starts, rather than after all work is completed. One option exercised here was an expanded kitchen that absorbed the den—instead of two separate rooms. A fine Welch dresser becomes the centerpiece of this charming cocktail/ dining area.

expanded
kitchens

Noting that visitors spent a great deal of time in the kitchen, architect Kenneth L. Smith and wife, Beth, designed a radical living room for their new house. This "living room" (*left*) is a dramatic two-story space that encompasses all the kitchen necessities as well as a dining table and fireplace. Perched above this is a desk and work area—a great vantage point for keeping an eye on activities around the house. The Smiths were their own builders; they even constructed the handsome curved counter top, using 1 by 4-inch oak strips.

An imaginative breakfast area (*right*) was designed and built by another ambitious couple, Bryan and Beverly Griffiths. The mullioned windows, stained-glass details, and oak-and-vinyl flooring create a virtual conservatory of light and plants just steps from the kitchen work area. The space seems to have a magnetic quality . . . everyone migrates to it from all over the house.

the total space: serenity

Often it's important to create a striking contrast between a private
environment and the world outside. One way is to establish total serenity,
an almost museumlike restraint that balances with frenetic city life.

In the heart of the desert the world without is sometimes harshly
brilliant, pressingly hot. Yet Mr. and Mrs. Norman Kreiss offer guests a
cool oasis in this gallerylike space in Rancho Mirage, California (*left*).
Walls are painted in pale gradations of cool color, and wicker and
other grasses add a note of controlled informality.

Designer David Carlson's approach is visual stimulation without
clutter (*above*). Carlson, an importer, designer, and collector, allows a
few fine artworks to dominate each space in his Los Angeles apartment.
Primitive and contemporary objects are manipulated to make a
personal statement. Here, amid found objects such as polished stones,
handmade baskets, chrome candlesticks, and Berber rugs, guests
experience a retreat from city noises and turn within for quiet conversation
or good music.

89

the total space: drama

Plump sofas, generously proportioned jars, puffy pillows, oak floors, and old beams . . . these are the ingredients designer Mark Paul mixes in this West Hollywood apartment to achieve a sense of drama (*left*). Nearly everything in the apartment was selected for its sculptural value. His collection of California pottery takes center stage and helps reduce the number of decorative objects needed for impact.

Even a small room can achieve a sense of drama with overscaled furnishings (*right*). Four-person sit-down dinner parties are compatible with the space limitations of Paul's apartment, although large numbers are often invited for buffet/tray lunches and brunches. A travertine-base dining table with a glass top is teamed with boldly proportioned Chippendale chairs for dramatic sculptural effect.

the total space: drama

Designed for people and art, this living gallery in the home of Mary and David Martin synthesizes the best spatial concepts of our time: grand space that doesn't overwhelm the human element. "We call this our studio," says David, "and it serves as an entertainment center." On the wall is a Lichtenstein banner made of plastic, canvas, and felt.

spatial freedom

Architects play a significant role in creating people-oriented spaces. But an aware client must lead the way. When an architect is his own client, the way is apt to be innovative, dynamic, and lively on a totally new level. Winter sun warms this greenhouse/sun room in the Santa Barbara home of architect Barry Berkus (above). The Berkus family enjoys the spatial freedom this sitting room offers, and they don't have to avoid the area during hotter summer months. Tall, deciduous trees, just outside the window wall, leaf out in early spring and by midsummer provide fresh green umbrellas of shade. It's a space designed for human comfort, not just for show, and also serves as a link in the passive solar-heating system.

It is possible to have a spatially exciting house that also provides private areas with doors, walls, and quiet corners (above right). Designed by architects Ellis D. Gelman and Gary L. Scherquist, the plan for Jan and David Blakemore's house began with a hillside site and evolved into a multilevel structure that embraces the drama and serenity they sought.

At lowest level is a recessed seating area with a massive fireplace wall; the next level features a bar; higher still is the kitchen and dining room. Lighting and music systems add special effects.

94

the total space: expanding horizons

The last glints of the sun signal the start of evening activities in the living room of jewelry designer Pepi Kelman (*above*). Starting with her two-bedroom, one-bath house in Malibu, Kelman expanded it in a skyward direction to provide needed guest space and to maximize the sea view. She and builder Jim Fikes of Danadesign Ltd. worked several years getting design changes approved by a strict coastal commission. The result is a fluid, spontaneous area where guests may choose the sea orientation or find more secluded spaces for reading or napping.

The sea and sky are the center of interest at interior designer John Cottrell's Laguna Beach house (*above right*). So he specified a neutral background of creamy beige and white for his easy mix of cotton-upholstered chairs and sisal carpeting. The whole game plan here is for feet-up comfort and easy-care surfaces. Wet feet, sand, pets, and people are part of the picture, and Cottrell takes them all in stride, with a no-nonsense formula for entertaining. People and pleasures take first priority here.

sleep

The need for shelter may actually begin with sleep. Most other activities can be performed in the open without anxiety or tremulous concern. But there is something especially vulnerable about the state of sleep. We must release conscious control of mind and body and allow nature's cyclic patterns to take over as our awareness dissolves into slumber.

Once we deliver ourselves to sleep we find that the body's night monitors are surprisingly efficient: lungs perform, heart beats, blood circulates, skin and cells continue to discard and restore tissue—all without our willing it.

Yet there is a subliminal awareness of the kinship between sleep and death, and it is therefore understandable that we humans surround the hours of slumber with multitudinous bits of ceremony and ritual. One remembers the prayer of childhood: "If I die before I wake, I pray the Lord my soul to take." With such a sendoff how could most of us avoid "dressing" for sleep? The bath or shower, hairbrushing, clean nightgarments, fragrant powders—perhaps they are preparation for those hours of communicating at another level of understanding. Is "I'll see you in my dreams" a real possibility as well as a song title?

There's also the joyous awakening to consider. Each return to consciousness, whether from a long slumber or short nap, is like the beginning of a new life. We start afresh, sometimes having left behind or worked through a problem in our sleep, sometimes knowing we've been restored, and are better able to cope with whatever the day may bring.

Sleep may be supported in many ways. In some tropical countries, a simple rope hammock is the newlyweds' first matrimonial possession. Babies around the world are rocked in wooden or canvas cradles resting on the floor or in baskets suspended from a ceiling beam.

Mattresses of the nineteenth- and twentieth-century household have been tufted, quilted, decorated, fitted with springy coils, then dressed with finery fit for a royal couch. Woven grasses, air, water, and all manner of natural and synthetic mattings have been used to provide total body support for sleeping adults.

To some people the bed is a retreat, to others it is a stage—yet to everyone the bedroom is a very private place, whether it is used by one person or shared. *My* bedroom. *Our* bedroom. Never *the* bedroom. It is often the most revealing room in our lives.

Setting the stage for sleep, a canopied bed has become an important architectural element in a sleek urban apartment. Designed by Judith Wilson for a condominium in Century City, California, this lofty unit expresses a number of design refinements of the modern bed.

more than sleep:
retreat for guests

The space was architecturally commanding (*left*),
yet owners Eileen and Norman Kreiss did not want
their second-story retreat to lack human scale and
warmth. So in the mini living room section of their
master suite they used a flow of soft-edge forms such
as their Malibu chaises, peach-colored table, and
round, lacquered mirror. Even the bed and its head-
and footboards have been upholstered in puffy
quilted coveralls. Guests are often invited upstairs to
partake of cocktails and appetizers in front of the
bone-warming fire.

There's a sitting-room quality to this guest bedroom
(*right*), where a visitor can spend quiet hours away
from general household activity. Although it's on
the highway side of the Kreiss's Malibu home, it still
seems remote from frantic resort activities. Tiered,
lacquered trunks imported from China add stack-up
storage space for bed linens and other amenities.
Wicker chairs and tables make pleasing companions
to the pecky cypress walls. The architect was Douglas
Rucker, A.I.A.

more than sleep: the bedroom

During daylight hours it is nice to have an open-door policy about bedrooms. They can provide extra pockets of comfort and beauty for residents and friends.

In remodeling a thirty-nine-year-old house in West Hollywood (*above*), art gallery owner Leo Duval made two rooms from one and created this dramatic area where paintings share starring credits with seating and sleeping arrangements. After having lived with hardier colors, Duval agreed with designer John Patton that he should exchange boldness for tranquillity. Soft beigy tones now provide perfect light-balance for this gallerylike space.

When sleep is the *raison d'être* for a bedroom, all attention may focus on that inviting object, the bed. Reaching beyond the bedroom walls for design inspiration, Wayne Kirts, A.S.I.D., keyed this pine platform bed to the desert terrain outside (*right*). Mr. and Mrs. Alan Moskowitz requested only that their condominium in Palm Desert, California, be designed around a natural and simple theme. The space is decorated with local rocks, American Indian baskets, natural weeds, and birch branches. Contemporary lamps and luxurious bed linens lend polish to the semirustic aspect of the rough-hewn four-poster.

more than sleep: beauty and practicality

A gleaming brass bed in an unusual four-poster design adds lustrous life to this charming setting designed by Betty Willis, A.S.I.D. (*left*). The classic boudoir theme began with C.W. Stockwell's "Gretchen" wallpaper and matching fabric; custom pillow shams and coverlet take full advantage of the border motif in this floral-stripe pattern. A chair and ottoman provide comfortable seating for this bedroom.

When L. Jarmin Roach and Karl Copas, both A.S.I.D., decided to share a townhouse in Newport Beach, California, they faced one major problem: how to merge two personal collections of furnishings, art, and accessories into one contemporary interior. Their solution was a triple-duty bedroom (*right*) that houses a collection of framed etchings, a work-at-home desk and chair, and a spacious upholstered daybed that doubles for nighttime sleep. All elements are held together with a desert-tan color scheme.

the art of sleep

Bedrooms needn't be filled with traditional appurtenances. Turn an artist loose in the bedroom and you'll discover an original approach to furnishing the space. In this bedroom (*above*), an Ellsworth Kelly painting, kachina dolls from American Indian cultures, and an early American quilt successfully mingle with other possessions in a striking composition.

If sleeping is an art, perhaps the greatest sleeping place in the art world was conceived by Jim Tigerman for a bedroom in Leo Duval's former condominium (*right*). Puffed-and-stuffed-canvas forms like soft rocks surround a double-platform bed, and two soft-sculpture palm trees stand at its head. There's even a tiny soft-sculpture airplane tucked in among the palm fronds.

artist in the bedroom

Walls aren't the only surfaces crying out for embellishment. Here simple stencils add charm and versatility to a rustic bedroom that could work as easily in a city home (left).

Most of us connect cheery floral patterns and pine furnishings to our earlier country cousins. Thrifty pioneers knew how to turn to advantage everything that came their way, and if they couldn't afford a rug they painted one on the floor. In this setting designer Carl Briant borrows that idea to re-create a country look with a French flavor. He custom designs a pine four-poster, then adds floor stenciling inspired by the background pattern in the bed linens (above).

Floor stenciling is easy once the decorative motif is selected. In this case, first the design was scaled up on a piece of tracing paper, then transferred to heavy-duty stencil paper. The floor was painted bright blue, then when dry the stencil was positioned and the motif filled in with white paint. After the pattern was completely painted and dried, the floor was given a coat of clear sealer. For additional helpful advice about floor stenciling, turn to page 30.

109

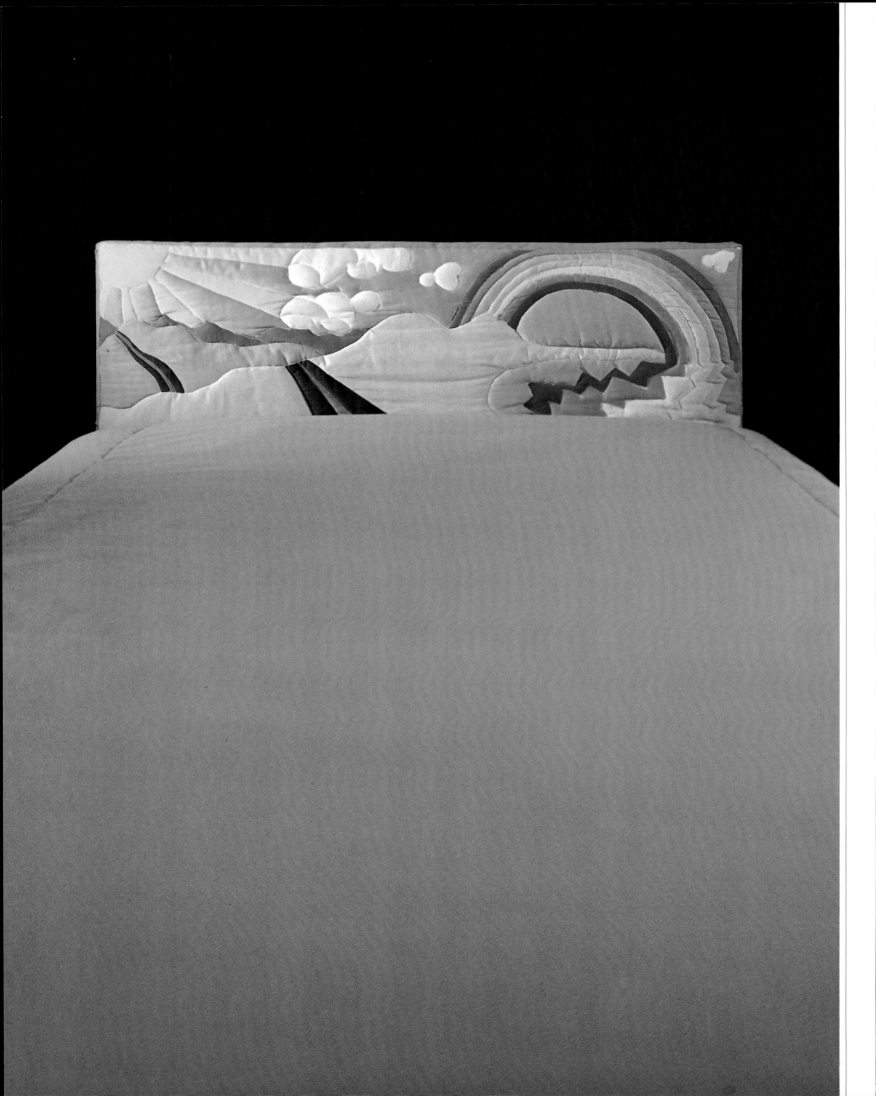

artist in the bedroom:
thread, ink, and paint

Bedrooms offer endless opportunities for creativity: they invite us to develop them as private displays of personal talents.

For a fresh and easy approach to do-it-yourself bed dressing, Ruth and Brian McKinney suggest a Land of Oz scenic slipcover for a headboard (*left*). Although the McKinneys hand painted the fabric, a similar result could be achieved by quilting a commercially printed fabric. Outline stitching, or quilting, creates a cushioned, three-dimensional effect, and a matching green coverlet leads the eye directly to the enchanted road of sweet dreams.

Rainbows are always a popular and easily executed motif for walls (*above*). Carol Isenberg has carried out her son's request and has interpreted a boldly banded rainbow painted directly above the trundle bed in his room.

islands for sleep: platform beds

One of the newest, most liberating concepts in the world of sleep is the island, or platform, bed. No longer must furnishings be positioned against the wall—now a bed may stand on its own, center stage.

Promoting the bed to a more prominent position in the bedroom does cause one problem: it has to be appealing when seen from all four sides. Fortunately, today's bedding manufacturers are helping to solve this in-the-round visibility. In the setting shown here the bedclothes have a special flair from every angle. As designed by Ristomatti Ratia, the bedding has some new wrinkles: pillowcases are continental style with envelope ends that fold neatly out of sight, while the polyester-filled comforter slips inside a fitted coverlet, called a *duvet*.

platform beds

Fresh air, curtain-free windows, and an island platform bed that seems to float is the formula for year-round comfort in this Pasadena house (*left*). Designed by Jerry Balest and Steve Fife, the diagonally placed bed allows access to balcony, storage space, and closets. Instead of curtains for the windows, the team used latex paint, a hand-cut stencil, and a small paint roller to create "etched" windowpanes.

When the surge of fresh ideas in designs for sleep seems to come to a halt, there is often someone ready to renew that flow. For example, a team of architects in a New York-based firm called Natural Selections daydreamed about new uses for corrugated and came up with a platform bed created entirely of cardboard (*above*). They fashioned this sturdy knock-down bed out of double-weight board. Cardboard ribs are slotted to allow easy assembly, and a boxlike frame cantilevers over the base for a professional look.

almost outdoors

Were it not for animals and insects, many of us would enjoy sleeping in the garden beneath a treed canopy. Even so, there are ways to re-create that garden mood indoors without disturbance from nature's creatures.

Dramatizing the lush quality of Hawaii's tropical greenery, the owners of this house in Haiku Plantations on the island of Oahu opted for this window-wrapped space (*above*). Bands of louvered and screened apertures allow fresh, scented breezes to enter, and each morning there's a view of this opulent foliage. Designed by architect Robert M. Fox, A.I.A., for Marvin K. Devereux and William Prange, Jr., this house nestles on a verdant site on the windward side of the island.

One of man's earliest sleep inventions was the hammock. There's a classic purity in its design, and a functional honesty. It's ideal for hot climates, allowing breezes to circulate from below. The slightest body motion causes it to swing gently. This triple-hammock lanai setting (*right*) is in the João Cauduro home in Brazil's resort area of Fortaleza Bay.

waterbeds

The water-filled mattress was perhaps the most revolutionary sleep idea to emerge in this century. And it all started as a student project in 1969. The dreamer? Charles Hall.

It's still too soon to draw any conclusions about the place waterbeds will take in the history of home furnishings, but they have made a mark on this latter part of the twentieth century. Although Hall, an American, conceived the waterbed and worked to develop the first model, other designers from around the world picked up his lead. A sumptuous version is made in France for Roche Bobois (*left*). Upholstered in luxurious deep red suedes, it has its own matching bedside tables that slide easily into place.

Two great bed ideas in one (*right*): twin waterbeds are supported by storage platforms in Laguna's Campaigner line.

beds for babies

It's hard to be objective about
babies. It's equally difficult to plan
appropriate environments for the
about-to-be-born. Some tykes
bubble with exuberance; others are
more reserved and observant, acting
like wise old owls from the first
moment they look around.
For example, vivacious Kelly
was a heavenly baby from birth, so
the sky-blue and cloud-patterned
comforter, sheet, and crib bumper
are perfect for her white-painted
spool crib. Designed by Ruth
and Brian McKinney, the line,
called Beautiful Dreamer,
cleverly includes coordinated
pillow slips for the bed
and T-shirts and panties
for its lucky occupant.

Shannon is sitting pretty on a hand-sewn quilt created from broad taffeta and grosgrain ribbons. From McKinney Art Studios in Venice, California, this design can be easily reproduced by even the novice seamstress. Bright ribbons in widths from two to six inches have been sewn together and attached to fabric backing. The space between is then filled with polyester batting.

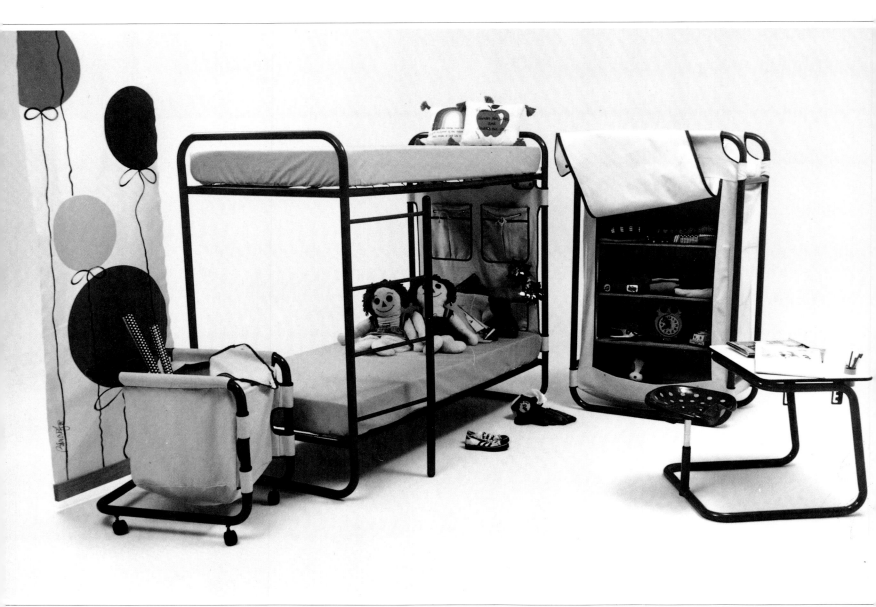

lively lairs for kids

Kids are climbers—they reach, fall back, then reach again. As soon as it's safe, why not offer them some two-story lairs? You'll be providing an environment for creative play and intriguing pre-sleep.

Youngsters are inventive, but they aren't likely to concentrate their attention on one thing for more than a few minutes at a time. When designer Marc Berthier began working out ideas for a line of furniture for children, he made sure the design concepts would fascinate a youngster. This two-level tubular bed finished in colorful baked enamel (*left*) engages kids in the same way that monkey bars do. Canvas pockets hang on one end of the structure, providing handy spots for books and small toys. Canvas flaps conceal storage shelves in an étagère; a canvas catch-all on casters acts as a mobile storage bin or hamper. There's also a tractor-type seat that grounds the active artist for extra minutes of artwork. Made in France for Roche Bobois, the line is called Twenty Tube.

Bright blue and yellow tubular bunk beds, called Big Toob (*right*), are the focus of this space-age bedroom. These unusual forms become the take-off point for a child's space fantasies. Part of a line of visionary furnishings for children, they were designed by Jim and Penny Hull for their firm, H.U.D.D.L.E.

lively lairs for kids

Here are two ways to induce youngsters to tuck in for the night, and
each has its daytime drawing power. A bedroom in a 1920's California
bungalow belonging to designers Jim and Penny Hull is treated to some
pow color (*above*). Taking center stage is the team's unique answer to a
twenty-four-hour sleep and playspace—the Huddlecouch. Wrapped in
Penny Hull's bull's-eye fabric, the canvas sling structure provides a
special retreat for kids. Window shades have been fringed with brilliant
sunset hues, thanks to that same bold fabric.

When Helen Reddy and Jeff Wald bought their house, an unfinished
shell of a structure sat in the backyard just waiting to be transformed.
With designer Sharon Landa's help, the Walds created this family
get-together space (*right*). At one end there's a three-story loft fitted with
mattress-size pads. Antique fire ladders and brass poles encourage
youngsters to make exciting firehouse-style slides from the upper story.
Walls have been surfaced in rough-sawn cedar laid in a herringbone
pattern. What a setting for a slumber party!

124

the art of keeping

A hundred times a day each of us makes two choices: discard or keep, toss or save. The moment we acquire a new object or decide to keep an old one for another day, a problem arises: how to store each element so it will be easily retrievable for future use.

There is an art to storing useful as well as beautiful objects. Some techniques must be developed through trial and error. Many lessons come from the past. Storage containers are almost always found among the artifacts of early cultures. Such primitive receptacles as gourds, shells, earthenware pots, and amphorae were stored in cool subterranean caves; varieties of baskets, woven specifically as containers, were suspended from roof structures to allow air to circulate and also served as lightweight portable receptacles well suited for transport by foot or animal caravan. In the Orient, wood-and-lacquer modular boxes and chests were utilized for small spaces and rough sea transport. These are imitated today in the form of campaign chests and modern tonsu that stack three or four feet high. The American Shakers lined their walls with pegs. From these were hung every kind of possession—towels, hats, and even chairs.

With such a wealth of human experience, we should now be proficient in this art of keeping and retrieving. Yet, inevitably, we seem more adept at acquisition than disposition. When such strain is placed on existing space, it becomes increasingly difficult to establish open areas for human activities.

Many "keeping" needs are tied to special interests—gourmet cookery, music appreciation, woodcrafting, sewing, creative stitchery, and wine tasting—as well as support systems for these activities, which frequently include books, tools, and sophisticated equipment. Add personal needs to household requirements and it's easy to understand why storage should be given top priority in space planning.

Practical storage facilities for a family needn't imitate factory warehousing. Each space needs its own formula. Some things should be within arm's reach—books, tapes and records, drinking glasses, pots and pans. Other items are better behind closed doors—luggage, linen, clothing, documents, grooming aids.

Whatever the choice, the goal is retrievability. And once that goal is attained, the ongoing task is to weed out, refine, and discard unused items or to relegate them to a less accessible level of storage.

With a bow to Thomas Jefferson's inventive genius, a nod of approval to architects Frank Lloyd Wright and Greene and Greene for their concepts of built-in storage, and with appreciation to George Nelson and Charles and Ray Eames, the twentieth-century visionaries who conceived what we now call wall systems, we present the ways in which many contemporary families master the art of keeping.

An array of baskets is suspended from the exposed Douglas fir beams in the all-wood house of Mr. and Mrs. Dick Rice. An idea borrowed from the past, this storage system allows access for everyday use and at the same time dramatically displays their fine basket collection.

exposed storage: collections

Favorite possessions: some of us don't wish to be separated from them; we want to be able to reach out and touch them, or at least to cast a glance in their direction for instantaneous pleasure.

The art collector develops a keen eye and a certain pride in discovering one special object in a shop full of ordinary wares. But as the discoveries mount, so does the need to draw attention to each of these treasures. Museum curator and folk-art specialist Joseph Terrell is involved in just such a love affair with books, baskets, pottery, and rugs. And by placing them in artful arrangements within arm's reach—on walls, floor, tables, and seating—he establishes a living collection that is totally integrated into his two-level condominium.

exposed storage: kitchens

See-through glass panels replace standard cabinet doors in the kitchen of Gail and Barry Berkus (*above*). Sweeping reforms for the kitchen were made as architect Berkus followed guidelines established by Gail and their three children. One convenient feature is the track lighting system that allows pinpoint adjustments as needs change. The storage island doubles as a serving buffet and houses a battery of spices and a partial collection of table wines.

When a family of cooks converges on the kitchen, there's bound to be competition for the choice workspaces. That's one conflict Sheila and Michael Ricci wanted to avoid when they began the expansion of their small kitchen. With the help of Myron Prudian and Associates, an unused bedroom and laundry were redeveloped to provide space for this gathering room (*right*). The Riccis decided on a mix of exposed and enclosed storage and a large center island that would allow them to share food-preparation chores. Overhead racks, undercounter niches, and a series of freestanding devices lighten some of the storage workload.

filing systems for the home

Just about every household has a linen closet and a separate closet for cleaning aids. But many new families have decided to bring together in one well-organized space all the ingredients needed for bed, bath, and good grooming.

Bedding, sewing gear, soaps, bathroom tissues, towels, sundries, and a roll-around cart nestle together in this bedroom-wing closet that has become a miniature keeping room. The family quartermaster can issue refills and freshly laundered items from this handy staging area. If the laundry equipment is nearby, the management gets four stars for excellence.

the organized refrigerator

To achieve the ultimate in cold storage many families are rethinking how freezer and refrigerator space is being used. Anyone can take a lesson from the fast-food industry and organize.

This side-by-side refrigerator/freezer (*right*) is a super sophisticate by Sub-Zero, but even *it* may be improved through the introduction of a color-coding system for the contents of meat and vegetable drawers. Shiny chrome bins may be added to the freezer compartment, air-tight storage jars and snap-on slings can be inserted for cheese, wine, and canned beverages. Wine glasses and party foods, such as a chocolate mousse cake, can be speedily chilled in the freezer.

By varying the heights of containers and by using see-through accessories it's possible to upgrade the visual appeal as well as the function of any refrigerator. Best of all, when fresh foods are easily accessible and visible, waste is reduced.

getting technical

A good storage system should free us for more interesting pursuits. In the planning stage we need not think that the systems must be complex to get the job done. A simplified work/dining center has been created from this late twentieth-century version of the old kitchen worktable *(below)*—but now it's made with sawhorse-type supports and has a tractor-seat stool as its working companion. Everything comes apart for storage or for a move to tomorrow's

home base. These Carefree Livin' designs have related storage systems that may be fitted with high tech wire baskets and plastic-coated bins to suit individual needs. Even the lighting fixture is a factory-inspired concept.

When you think that every available space has been filled, look again—there is probably more. Maybe there's a hall wall that hasn't been put to the test. A wire grid system *(right)* by Hodges High Tech and the system *(far right)* from The Design Source, Inc., may be used in multiples from floor to ceiling; each will make little intrusion on walking space in a narrow corridor or passageway.

getting technical

There's a growing interest in the prefabrication of a variety of storage components for the kitchen and other areas of the house. Versatile enough to accommodate any theme from "country" to "modern," they are ready to install and come packaged with hardware and instructions.

The handsome cabinets shown here are fitted with an amazing selection of efficiencies that may be ordered from the factory for a truly individualized kitchen. This system, designed for Allmilmo in West Germany, helps solve problems when creating new kitchens or remodeling old ones. Lisbeth and Loch Jones and a team from Kitchen Design specified such features as a pull-out pantry and ventilated vegetable drawers. Finger grips and toe spaces add functional elegance to the line.

for listening and looking: media rooms

When the quality of listening is involved, music lovers don't want to commit the reproduction of sound to a period piece. Video buffs also want to keep up with technological advances by selecting storage shells that can be changed to accommodate new equipment.

Bunny and Dick Orkin wanted clean, sweet sound in a comfortable setting *(right)* rather than a dazzling array of dancing digitals and frenzied meters reminiscent of a recording studio. They also needed generous seating with good body support for guests and family members who would be settling in for an evening of critical listening and/or viewing. Since Orkin is half of the popular and zany team of radio characters known as Dick and Bert, he required a high level of sophistication in the equipment and its storage. The result, designed by Mark Paul, was an upholstered niche and ten-foot-high lacquered cabinets with doors that hide the hardware.

Wires and plugs are all part of the *raison d'être* for sophisticated sound. In the Logus system *(above)*, designed by Janine Roze, industrial-type slotted shelving supports a series of metal storage trays. This enables the audiophile to manipulate equipment so that a high degree of perfection can be obtained. Designer Teri Fox injects black ribbon-tufted seating into the scene for easy listening.

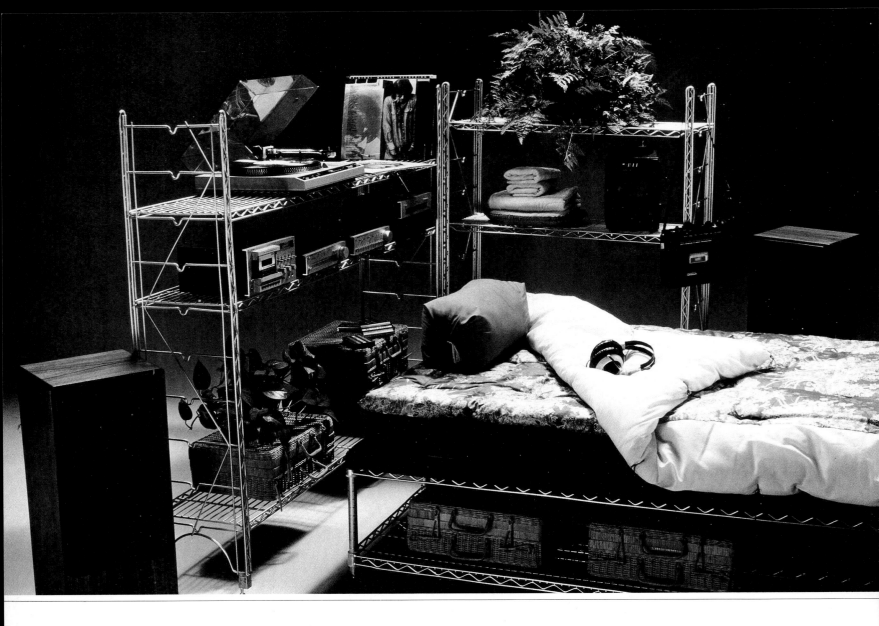

audio centers

One-room living may be a necessity for many discriminating listeners, yet few will want to sacrifice good sound no matter how tight the space. In this arrangement (*above*), a platform bed and pair of shelf systems by Erecta and Super Erecta provide quality listening while gracefully recognizing the realities of living in reconstructed spaces.

Compact wood components by Music Waggon (*right*) are an attractive solution for anyone who wants to snuggle up to his or her favorite sounds.

audio centers simplified

For the broadest possible listening experience at home, various kinds of equipment may be brought together in an interesting way.
A solid oak audio center supports wood-finish components in this setting by Mel Brown (above).

The joy of listening outranks most other activities in this artist's loft (right). Bedding is simplified in the Japanese style, with a futon fold-away mattress, roll-up comforter, and tatami floor covering, all of which work well with screens and a lamp designed by L.A. Shoji. These traditional Japanese elements are combined with triangular-shaped storage stack-ups that act as a room divider. Music-lover Mel Brown chose this knock-down system for its tinker-toy precision; it can be assembled into dozens of unique configurations.

wall systems

Accessibility—that's the key word for the space designer Teri Fox has put together (*left*). A herringbone-quilted sofa, red mover's quilt, and white Parsons table stand solidly before a transparent wall system fitted with television, miniaturized stereo components, and video-game attachments. As an appropriate decorative element, framed panels of a fabric printed with a computer-circuit pattern are used.

Domani lacquered-wood hookups (*above*) are yet another elegant way to house a music system. Shelves may be flip-flopped as shown to provide sculptural interest.

artists' spaces

Fiber artist and weaver Carole McCarty, her architect husband, Harrell, and their son, Morgwn, live on a rain-swept site near Hawaii Volcanoes National Park. Instead of packing all living and working spaces under one roof, the McCartys chose a three-structure complex. In Carole's private workshop (*left*), floor-to-ceiling shelves, handcrafted by Harrell, hold her collection of yarns and baskets conveniently near her handmade teak loom. This carefully planned work/storage area reveals the family's pervading desire to find beauty in utility. Architects were Oda/McCarty of Hilo.

There is an art to swapping and recycling objects, and the first talent required is the ability to recognize quality in off-beat objects and other people's discards. The second talent is the capacity to organize these collectibles without diminishing the joy of keeping them in view. The highly personalized dining area of two artists, Diana and Dennis Miller, is a case in point (*right*). They have taken this low-rent loft in the inner city and converted it into an eye-grabbing, comfortable home and studio. Dozens of good finds mingle with handmade items, such as Dennis's stained-glass lamp and Victorian-doily pillows. Diana's artwork merges photographs and tearsheets that record events in the lives of people they admire.

the live-in gallery

Perhaps the home has always been a private gallery—a space where we reveal ourselves through our preferences in furnishings, art, and collectibles. The passion for exploring, in depth, one facet of our culture, is reflected in the home of Mr. and Mrs. Peter Sidlow. Their commitment is to advertising art, and their collection includes dozens of lithographed items: tobacco tins, talcum-powder cans, printer's trays, imprinted hand mirrors, promotional give-aways, and colorful store-display materials. This phenomenal assortment has been meticulously inventoried, then collated into flat drawers, glass-enclosed cupboards, and open shelving, with space left over for wall art. Architects Matlin and Dvoretzky, A.I.A., and designer Don Martin shaped the house to fit the collection, rather than the other way around.

workshop for a carpenter

This super workshop is a woodworker's dream. It could inspire any handy person to pull up his socks and begin to make order out of chaos. It all started innocently as Thomas C. Goodacre set out to organize his garage and workshop. One thing led to another and before he realized it he had created a strikingly well-composed space where heavy-duty jobs as well as simple ones can be executed. By utilizing his impressive collection of secondhand power tools, Goodacre crafted compartmentalized drawers for nails, bolts, and hardware, and brought order to the usual disarray of pliers, wrenches, and drill bits. There's even a vacuum system for quick cleanup. His workbench is surfaced in oak flooring salvaged from a school gymnasium. For convenience and safety, one key operates all locks.

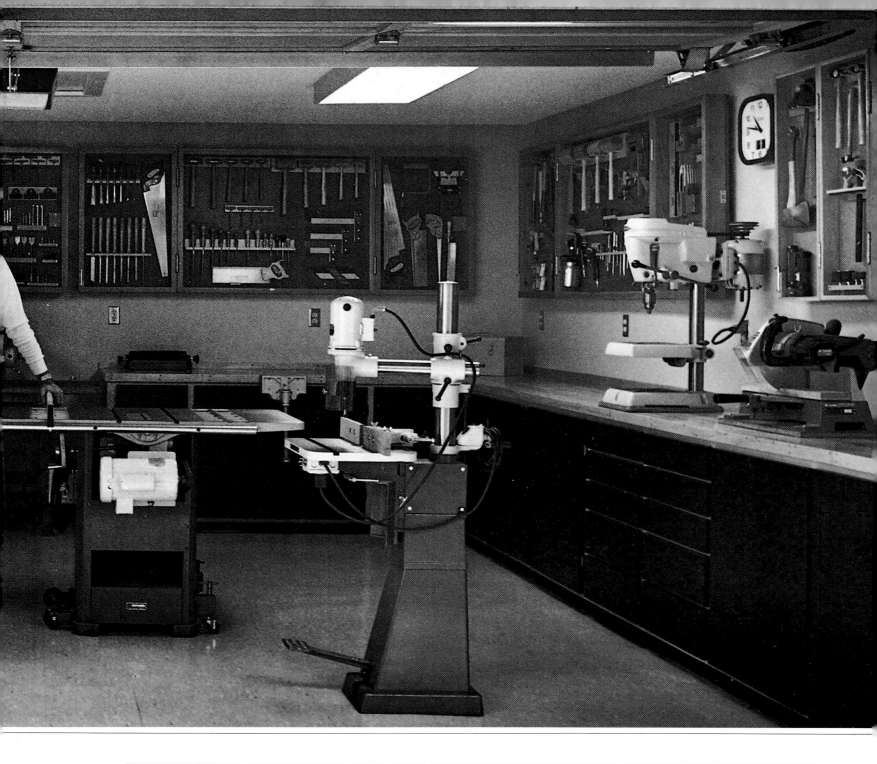

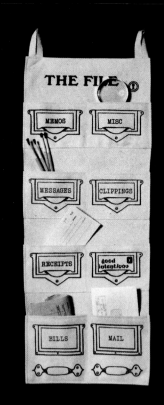

space stretching

Little things add up—vitamin pills, spices, toiletries, jewelry, buttons and bows. When possessions begin to possess us, we should consider new stash systems. It is possible to store thousands of tiny components so they can quickly be retrieved —it just takes a few hours of planning.

Designer Edna Sheldon suggests keeping an eye on rubber bands, stamps, pastry points, and dozens of "must haves" by using stacking plastic boxes in assorted sizes (*left*).

Freelance writer Laurie Gottlieb opts for soft canvas packaways (*above right*). Their handy pockets expand to hold such items as catalogues, small magazines, keys, and tools.

Finally, Jill Flynn selects an array of natural pine racks (*below right*) whose bold lines lend themselves to decorative display.

mini mail room

Much of the attention given to housing our personal possessions stems from a simple basic need—convenience. And when such items are handy, the chances are great that we will use them more. How often have you put off letter writing because the scramble for stationery and stamps seemed like too much trouble? Gift packaging is equally troublesome when you have to dig for ribbon, paper, and tape, then clear a space for the wrapping process.

Love is one of the reasons we devote so much time to gift wrapping and letter writing. Our time is a gift of love; the papers and ribbons are an embellishment.

At the request of editors of the Los Angeles Times *Home* magazine, designers Ruth and Brian McKinney recently devised the ultimate solution: a miniature mail room for the house. Forty-eight inches wide and hung from the wall, the unit has a decorative drop leaf that opens to reveal its own support—a frame-shaped leg.

Slots have been created for all family wrapping and writing needs, and there is a series of inset "mail cans" for intrafamily communication. For instructions on how to duplicate this convenient home work center, please turn the page.

constructing a mini mail room

Simple lumber and a few paint colors enable even the novice woodworker to re-create this wall-hung wrapping center.

MATERIALS

kiln-dried no. 2 grade knotty pine

1 48-inch dowel, ¼ inch in diameter

4 30-inch dowels, 1 inch in diameter

1 box finishing nails

4 1½ by 2-inch solid brass hinges

2 brass leg brace hinges

carpenter's glue

6 gluing clamps

miter box and clamps

15-200 garnet sandpaper

150 wet/dry carborundum sandpaper

1 can wood putty (to match color of pine)

coping saw, circular saw

electric jigsaw, electric drill

carpenter's square

1 quart white pigmented shellac

1 can acrylic-base white primer spray paint

pint cans of high-gloss interior latex paint

1 can Deft wood sealer

masking tape

Note: To support the dowels that hold the rolls of wrapping paper it's necessary to create small wooden holders. In six 1¾ by 2½-inch blocks of pine, drill a 1¼-inch hole ⅜ inch deep. Then saw two blocks on the diagonal. Each dowel will lock into one full and one half support.

When preparing exterior surfaces for paint, sand first with garnet sandpaper then with carborundum paper. Be sure to shellac all knots before priming. Allow paint to dry between coats at least twenty-four hours and mask painted surfaces only after seventy-two hours.

BASIC FRAME: 1

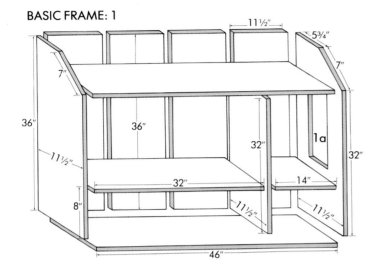

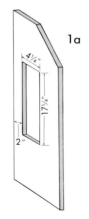

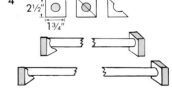

ADDING SHELVES: 2

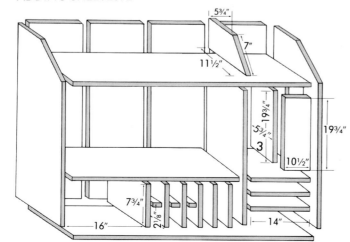

FINISHING SHELVES: 5

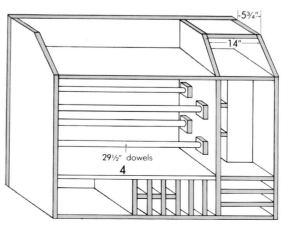

TABLE SUPPORT: 6

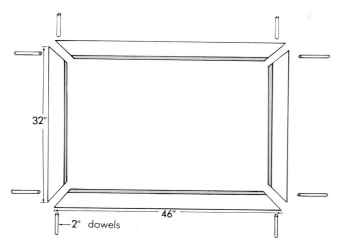

32"

46"

2" dowels

TABLETOP ASSEMBLY: 7

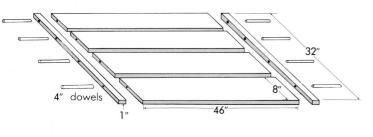

4" dowels

1"

46"

8"

32"

1   Lay four 11½ by 36-inch boards on large flat surface. Apply glue and clamp. Dry for 24 hours. Cut two side panels and mark 32 inches up from bottom. Use a circular saw to cut a 45-degree angle from mark.

1a   On one side panel measure two inches from rear edge; trace a 4¼ by 17¼-inch rectangle. Cut with circular saw, finish corners with coping saw. Sand, glue, and nail side panels to back. Cut and attach bottom board. Cut and affix 32-inch vertical divider. Assemble remaining horizontal shelves.

2   Cut and attach all vertical and horizontal dividers except partitions around hole. Check angles with carpenter's square.

3   Cut three wood triangles. Position and attach to 19¾ by 5¾-inch board. Attach to unit as shown in figure 2.

4   Construct supports for wrapping-paper rolls. Attach dowel supports; full circles on right, half circles on left.

5   Affix remaining horizontal shelf. After sanding the surface, countersink nails and fill holes with putty.

6   To make table support, cut two 1 by 3 by 46-inch boards and two 1 by 3 by 32-inch boards. Miter ends on a 45-degree angle using miter box, clamps, and coping saw. Drill ¼-inch holes as shown; insert glue and dowels. Clamp. Check frame with carpenter's square. Dry for 24 hours.

7   To make tabletop, cut four 8 by 46-inch boards, glue and clamp. Dry 24 hours. Trim to a width of 44 inches. Cut two 1 by 32-inch strips. Measure and drill ¼-inch holes three inches deep through strips into tabletop. Insert glue and dowels. Clamp and dry 24 hours. Trim protruding dowels.

8   Now sand tabletop and frame. Center hinges over joint of tabletop and frame. Trace hinge shape with soft pencil. Chisel out a depression so hinges are flush with wood. Sand.

9   To tabletop and box only, apply two coats of Deft.

10   Sand underside of table with wet/dry carborundum paper. Apply shellac to knots on frame and underside of table; dry. Prime and paint. Let dry 72 hours. Draw design with pencil. Mask with tape. Paint. Paint table support.

11   When dry, assemble all parts; anchor hinges, and drop painted coffee cans into place.

MOTIF PAINTING: 10

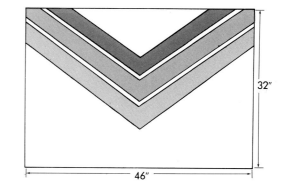

32"

46"

FINAL ASSEMBLY: 11

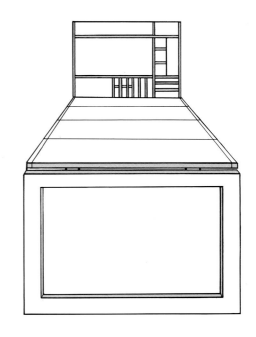

the bathing experience

The bathroom is the last private place, the great escape from household cares and family connections. The door closes behind us and, whether for one ten-minute period or one hour, we are free—finally *alone*.

It would be a mistake to assume that twentieth-century bathers have reached some new peak in environments for the bath. The Romans built luxurious public watering places, not only at home, but as far away as Bath, England, leaving behind a trail of conquered but presumably clean citizens. They placed importance on things physical, and much of the remaining Roman architecture reveals thermal systems designed to heat water and airspaces. The Romans created magic with water: fountains, streams, steamy vapors, and bubbling springs moved in a kinetic, perpetual flow.

Bathing is a tactile and sensual experience and most bathroom surfaces seem to heighten this sensuality. There is a slickness, a gloss, in products that reflect the characteristics of water—smooth porcelain, polished chrome, mirror, marble, ceramic tile, glass, brass. There is a special pleasure in the look and scent of wet wood. It is another practical, age-old material being used in today's bathroom. The Japanese *furo* is a good example. It can still be found in private homes in Japan and Hawaii.

There are some contributions to the art of the bath that can be credited to contemporary thinking. Foremost is the idea that the space be developed with uncompromising individuality. The bathroom wall becomes a gallery for the display of miniature prints, old menu covers, or wine labels. Shelves and counters are laden with dozens of seashells; magazine racks hold favorite reading materials. Just outside a door or window, in a pocket-size garden, are an open-air shower and exercise equipment.

Other recent contributions to the bathing environment come from manufacturers and designers who have, in the last five years, caused a revolution in the form of fixtures and fittings. Modern materials and technology bring us a palette of colors and finishes, setting the stage for small-space showmanship. Not all of these products have yet found their way into homes, but we show them here as an indication of the future.

The bathroom is a watery sanctuary where we change from our public selves to our private selves. We enter, stripped and unembellished, into this secluded place. We are alone, but never completely isolated from the things we love. Always there is an emotional connection reaching through the closed door, letting us know that once refreshed we may step back, with renewed vigor, into the world of shared activities.

A brick-encased bathtub, skylights, and a variety of trees and plants personalize this bathing sanctuary designed by Lee Poll and Ann Sterling.

sensuality with tile

Just as river waters carve the lands into sculptured contours, the tiles in this bath tease the senses with fluid implications of motion. A wall of mirror over the pristine countertop reflects an S-shaped tile niche. Within this recess, bathers step up to a shower on the first level or move to an elliptic tub on the higher level. There are no dividers here; splashed water can't hurt the tiles, and high-quality enamel paints have been used on wall surfaces. This unusual and undulating space is a tile-setter's masterwork. The curve-topped tiles are from L.A. Tile Co.

the naturalness of wood

The use of wood in a bathing place has practical reasons as well as esthetic ones. Naval architects and shipwrights have long understood the symbiotic relationship that exists between wood and water.

Some homeowners have the ability to synthesize and refine an idea down to its essential elements, an architectural philosophy expressed as "less is more." The design strength in this tripart space is its spare beauty. Designer Joan Stevens conceived this sauna/bath for her Hollywood Hills home, drawing upon a Nordic simplicity. From steam room to shower and grooming area, there is a continuity of materials and character: extraneous decoration is kept to a minimum.

wood, water, and steam

Wood wears well in a moist environment and provides a handsome setting for bathroom activities. This tub (*left*) is nicely incorporated into its wooden slipcover and receives the benefit of extra shelf space. A built-in cosmetic counter bridges two walls in this room designed by Linda Cracchiola.

When Richard Meyer remodeled a beach house, he decided to break with tradition and tuck a new hot tub into the front entry (*above*). One wall has been faced with rough-sawn cedar laid in a double-chevron pattern. Decorative tiles surface the two-level planting bed and line the step-in pool. Related quarry tiles pave the area. With insets of stained glass and diffused light from the skylights, there's definitely a romantic character to this unusual bathing facility that also serves as a reflecting pool.

modern design for the bathroom

Resembling molds for fine china, the sleek shapes of the plumbing fixtures in this bathroom are emphasized by horizontal elements (*left*). This design, by Sidney Altman, exhibits a totally self-sufficient approach. The sink counter is wall hung, leaving the floor area free. Other independent touches are the absence of a water tank for the toilet, the addition of storage space in the mobile vanity bench, the integration of towel bars into storage components, and the mirror with its self-contained lighting.

The tiles in the bath settings on this page are performing two roles. In the bathtub niche with the city skyline (*below*), inexpensive 4 by 4-inch tiles create a miniature mural. In this and other settings architect Gary Gilbar, A.I.A., uses tile graphics as a design signature.

Tiles molded of ABS plastic serve as containers for a variety of bathroom necessities that can otherwise cause clutter (*right*). Part of an extensive line called Quadrat made by Hammarplast of Sweden, the system encourages a form of storage gamesmanship—pocket tiles are placed wherever needed and snap on to adhesive-backed wall plates. Hooks, hangers, mirrors, towel racks, and tissue holders, available in green, wine, and brown, are included in the comprehensive system.

a bit of nostalgia

The mood is old world, the efficiency totally twentieth-century. A rich and elegant bathroom (*left*) was designed by Paul Donnell: brass carriage lamps flank the paneled mirror, gleaming wood tops the counter, and gold-plated faucets and basin add their luster. And just outside the French doors a tiny trellised garden awaits.

In an unusual case of recycling, designer Dolores Brucklmaier converted a fine old kitchen cupboard into a charming bathroom vanity (*right*). It's also a nice way to add a sink to a large bedroom—something European families have done for centuries.

new sculpture for the bath

A new generation of bathroom fixtures has been set before us in a delicious array of colors and surfaces. True sculpture for the bath, these fixtures show a reshaping of our attitudes about environments for grooming.

Opulent is the word for these slick, curvy forms in jewellike colors. Beautiful and functional, they come from the drawing boards of the great design houses of America and Europe. The American manufacturer, Kohler, offers sixteen tasteful colors. From others such as Richard-Ginori, Metallurgica, Piazza, and Balocchi of Italy we observe Ferrari-like refinements for sinks, faucets, and fittings. Ariete combines two-colors in vitreous-china entries.

new sculpture for the bath

Good design is spilling over onto bathroom hardware, and much to the delight of anyone about to upgrade an existing lavatory, faucet handles set the pace for a new look (*left*). The slick red and blue crisscross handles by Zazzeri are a tribute to the past and the present in their bold colors. Ferrari's famous stallion symbol embellishes Balocchi's chocolate-brown entry, while Sidney Altman's chrome-and-brass circle moves on to another plateau of design.

Architect and urban planner Jim Hull uses fused-on plastic coatings for his heavy-gauge steel bath accessories (*right and above*). Part of the H.U.D.D.L.E. line of Toobs, the group punctuates the direction bath fixtures are taking.

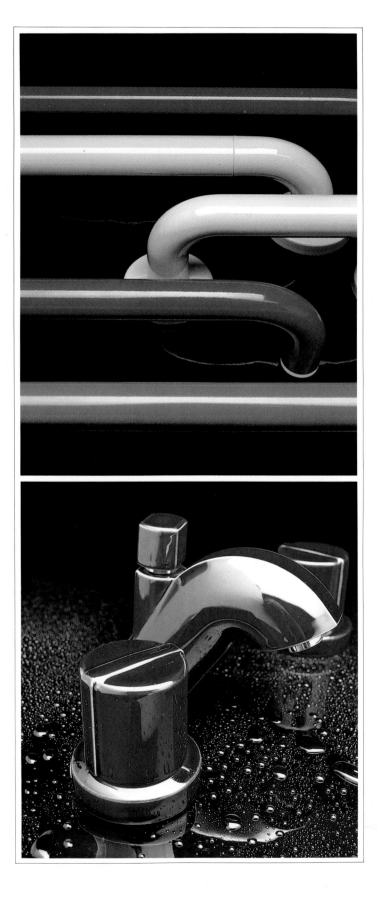

bathroom opulence

Malachite faucet handles with borders of polished chrome; storage areas concealed by mirrored Plexiglas; a plastic laminate that looks like brushed aluminum but is easier to care for . . . these are the materials that make this a flowing sculptural composition (*left*). A veritable work of art, this Waterfall Vanity, designed by Paul Associates, hits new heights of modern luxury with its nearly $4,000 (including malachite handles) pricetag.

The gleam of copper conveys a rich look of superb quality (*above right*). The hand-forged pure copper basin, imported from Mexico, is paired with a long-necked brass faucet, a variation on hospital hardware that was born at Chicago Brass. Sidney Altman contrived this smashing combination.

Based on an old Victorian design, this hand-held polished brass shower head continues to find a place in today's bathrooms (*right*).

beauty and body fitness

Attention to bathing, fitness, and personal grooming in environments that uplift the spirit should ultimately result in better health and a renewed *joie de vivre*. The bath can be more than the sybarite's retreat. It can be expanded to become a family home health center. When Barbara and Fred Miller began a fitness regimen it soon led to the development of this exercise room. With landscape architect Sid Galper, the Miller family created an all-encompassing space with tennis court, pool, spa, guest house, and entertainment area. Architect Robert L. Barnett, planned the exercise area *(left)*.

Ultimately each of us can jump for joy at our good fortune, achieve a rare control over mind and body. Our dancers rebound on Sundancer 38-inch trampolines.

water

Man has long had a desire to manipulate nature on a grand scale: redirect rivers, dam gentle green valleys and fill them with water, shore deltas to prevent flooding, and create lakes so that new houses may be described as "waterfront" or "lakeside." Even public places such as parks, stadiums, and golf courses have been planted with elaborate sprinkler systems in the belief that development of nonproductive land is as essential to our lives as food-producing agriculture and sea-harvesting aquaculture.

Water definitely is a companion to all living things. Water not only sustains life but enhances it, and many individuals find in it a natural therapy for mind and body. We have embraced the sauna, spa, hot tub, and swimming pool as addenda to good health and good living.

Architects and landscape designers have long acknowledged the relationship of water to architecture; some believe that fountains are architecture in motion. The water mirror, whatever its size, seems to double our vision and reach—part reality, part illusion. Water adds vitality to monumental structures, mirroring sculptural details we might miss at first glance.

Water is a renewable resource. Seldom "lost," it is ever in the process of conversion from liquid to solid to gas; from mist to steam to rain, snow, ice. Plants, people, and animals flourish in its presence. The sight of steam rising above an outdoor spa or hot tub promises delicious comfort and well being, while the splashing sounds of a miniature waterfall can lead us to deeper levels of contemplation and satisfaction in nature. Ours is a generation of water worshipers, and with a certain missionary zeal we have helped spread the word so that future generations around the world will find testimony in thousands of public and private watering places.

The spa is the latest addition to the American backyard. Smaller than a swimming pool and bigger than a hot tub, its popularity is due to the ease of installation and its versatility. Whether made of fiberglass, concrete, or wood, its jet streams of air circulate the water to create a pleasant sight and sound.

Today the spa has become a frequent companion to the pool, and this one, designed by Alan Ross for Carol and Jerry Isenberg, nestles into a garden planned by Mario Mathias and Loni Barnett.

181

water in the landscape

Before any dramatic vision can become a reality, the elements that make it effective must be understood. We are just beginning to rediscover the many ways water may be used in the man-made landscape.

Perched at what seems to be the edge of the world, this keyhole-shaped pool is about forty feet below the hilltop home of architect Paul Sterling Hoag, A.I.A. There's a sense of stark isolation from civilization—from telephone calls, neighborhood activities. As a result, swimming here is like visiting a remote resort. Between the pool and the hillside is an enclosed sauna; on the far side, facing the distant sea, is an untrammeled park preserve.

shaped to suit the site

Wraparound pools give owners room for swimming extra laps, but they also apparently lift houses out of the earth, giving the illusion of buildings floating, like barges on the water.

A steep slope left little room for a conventional swimming pool, but the owners wanted a stretch of water for serious swimming (*left*). The solution: wrap the pool around the house. Landscape architects Galper/Baldon and Associates created an eight-foot-wide, fifty-five-foot-long channel, culminating in a small, shallow cove with its built-in spa.

Taking a cue from sprawling, sunbleached Mediterranean villages, architect George Foy used water as though it were a miniature sea, to enhance and reflect this cluster of living spaces (*above*). There's a cliffside quality created by multilevel terraces that step down from rooftops to pool.

shaped to suit the site

There's something delightfully luxurious about a tiny beachside spa, this one designed by Frank Mascarelli (*above left*). The ocean is there to offer its dramatic waves and misty air as a backdrop to the redwood hot tub. This cozy area, nestled against a louvered redwood wall just outside the Malibu home of Steven Stewart, provides a warm contrast to that cool sea.

There were great granite boulders and a handsome Canary Island pine tree on the hillside site of Robert Evans's house (*below left*). Landscape architect Wiley Evans (son of the owner) built a long narrow pool bordered by ninety feet of redwood decking, without disturbing boulders or tree. The retaining wall against the hill establishes a mid-level area for a sunbathing deck and Jacuzzi. Twenty-five jets of water playfully cascade from the top of the wall.

This little jewel of a spa (*right*) was created completely by homeowner William Dorich, who installed the fiberglass shell and fixtures, and even poured the concrete and laid the brick for the surrounding terrace. A flat-plate solar collector on the garage roof heats the spa water to 85 degrees Fahrenheit. Natural gas then takes the temperature up to 100 degrees. At night a redwood deck covers the pool to prevent heat loss.

the natural haven

When the terrain has its own regal beauty, the addition of a pool or stream can double the impact of a natural site (*left*). There are many ways to fit water into a garden. A swimming pool would have been impractical on this sloping site, so the Robert Griffins chose a spa set in the deck on the lower level of their hillside house. Landscape architect Allen Fishman and architect John McInnes coordinated structural and natural elements into a sheltered green glade. The garden contains a cascading stream, rock garden, and hot-water soak tub. The latter is supported by a bed of sand and concrete footings just below the deck, to help carry the water's weight.

For a truly sybaritic setting, a gently sculpted wooden deck seems to float just a few feet above a hillside garden (*right*). Landscape architect Ray W. Forsum, A.I.L.A., dramatized the setting by adding wood framing that suggests an open gazebo. Although no actual roof separates bathers from trees, sky, rain, and fog, they enjoy a sense of privacy because shelter is implied. What a soothing pleasure it is to plunge into this tub of hot water on a decidedly cool evening or to luxuriate in the hammock stretched above it!

walkways to water

The way to the pool or spa can be as inviting as the destination itself, creating a ceremonious circuit from house to pool. The space between this house and its sundeck is roofed over by a wood lath shelter that casts dramatic patterns of sun and shadow on the short walk (*left*).

Wooden stairs and a two-level deck provide an attractive packaging for the redwood hot tub, designed by Wooden Environments for Bob and Julie Keller. Pumps and fixtures for the tub are neatly hidden in a covered wooden structure at the far end of the deck.

This trio of ceramic tile bathing fountains is contained by brick walkways (*right*). Designed by Dennis M. Taylor of the Peridian Group, it allows bathers to warm up in the high-temperature spa, cool down in the moderately heated plunge, and, for those who dare, a dash under the chilly waterfall. This award-winning concept was conceived for the home of Martin and Pauline Collins.

water and architecture

Some architectural situations demand the added dimension and enrichment of water. The rippling water in this grand pool (*left*) is sometimes transformed into mirrorlike calm, providing ever-changing images of the house with its thirty-foot silos. Designed by Barry A. Berkus, A.I.A., this family compound was completed over a period of several years. The whole house is responsive to nature. Solar-oriented heating and hot-water systems have been incorporated into all phases of the design, including the pool.

Dr. Jim Young of La Jolla, California, solved the problem of street noises with the design solution shown here (*below*). Designer Gary Stone, of Stone-Fischer & Assoc., installed a waterfall as the perfect mask for noise. Using the steep slope on Young's property, the designer created this powerful composition of retaining wall, waterfall, planting element, and two kinds of water. Night lighting adds a nice bit of flash.

water and architecture: the perfect companions

In 1968 architecture critic Dan MacMasters described this house in terms that foretold how ageless its design would prove to be: "This is the ultimate Palm Springs house. A house for this resort must be built for the desert. But it should be much more. It should be dramatic, charged with surprises . . . frankly self-indulgent . . . consummately finished. And it should be aloof enough to keep its character as the town sprawls off across the valley floor." Designed by architect John Lauter, A.I.A., for the late Arthur Elrod, the house described is developed around a series of circles and elliptical curves. The semicircular pool perches at cliff's edge, and its water level is so high that it appears ready to overflow. The fluid structural forms are of poured concrete, and one concrete wing supports a petallike roof that partially overhangs the pool.

195

glass, light, and color

One can easily sing the praises of plain, unembellished window glass: it is smooth and slick to the touch, surprisingly resilient, easy to keep clean, and a wonderfully transparent window on the world. It acts as windbreak, skylight, and ventilating device. A double layer of glass can be an effective insulation against the cold. It is an important functional element in contemporary architecture.

Apply the techniques of etching, scribing, leading, or coloring to that simple piece of glass and it is suddenly transformed, moving the viewer to a new level of perception. Even the descriptive vocabulary is different. The terms belong to the jeweler: facets, light refraction, clarity of color, opalescence. And as with jewelry, a semiprecious quality emerges in the final composition.

There are dozens of creative ways to use decorative glass, and many practical reasons for doing so. It can provide both light and privacy, hide an unsightly background, bring refracted color to a pristine interior. Although the true purpose of decorative glass is primarily to beautify, it also serves to surprise, delight, and uplift the viewer.

Whether designed as a permanent part of a structure or suspended in space, a decorative glass panel plays with natural light to enhance our perception of the volume contained within four walls. And natural light has its own rheostat, automatically attuned to the season and the hour.

Artificial light sources also exploit the best characteristics of decorative glass. Examples abound from the treasured works of Louis Comfort Tiffany to the contemporary dance floors of the disco generation—light and glass are well mated.

The most dramatic displays of decorative glass are generally assigned to gathering places—living rooms, entries, dining rooms, family kitchens. But many young families have begun to enjoy it in the secluded, private settings of bedroom or bath where decorative glass provides a kaleidoscope of intimately scaled pleasures. Miniature pools of pattern dapple the walls and secret rainbows travel mysteriously across the floors of these inner sanctums.

The glass treasure shown here was salvaged many years ago by designer artists Elizabeth and Tony Duquette. For a tiny pied-à-terre in San Francisco's Cow Hollow, they used this Louis Comfort Tiffany window as a background for desk work. The effect is doubled by a mirrored ceiling.

the ultimate illumination

This expanded space was created by Joseph and Bea Solomon from areas that were once small and boxy (*left*). Light-infusing skylights were added to the informal dining area after ceilings were raised to dramatic heights. The gallerylike setting showcases people and art in the most complimentary way.

In earthy contrast, a venerable carob tree framed by the geometric living room window dramatizes the Mike Evans house in Woodland Hills (*right*), while a skylight reveals the tree's branches.

the glazier's repertoire

The techniques of leaded glass were established through hundreds of years of work by master craftsmen: glass has been treated to meticulous etching, handsome beveling, and rich or delicate coloring. And the same choices exist today.

One spectacular work of etched and beveled glass was custom designed to suit the tastes of Charles and Norma Hester (*above and left*). The dragon theme evolved from their lifelong devotion to oriental masterpieces. Glass artists Tom and Gail Henry executed the intricate work, a pair of doors, over a three-month period. Even those who have seen the panels many times continue to be struck by the intense beauty of late afternoon sunlight as it is refracted by the glass.

A classic motif for stained and leaded glass is the rose. This example (*right*) is a contemporary interpretation by Bryer-Frank Studios that uplifts this street-side location.

color from above

Stained-glass ceiling panels suffuse a room with color and exquisite patterns of light. This ceiling, inspired by Victorian-era motifs, combines hand-painted glass with multifaceted "jewels" and opalescent fragments (*left*). Designed by Diana Bryer-Frank, it brightens a Pacific Palisades kitchen.

Another lavish kitchen installation (*right*) was made by Knight Studios for homeowner Bob Tamkin. Framed in wood and lit from above by low-watt bulbs, the panel may be dimmed or brightened by the turn of a rheostat. Bill Putney worked with Tamkin on the concepts for this remodeled kitchen.

accents for architecture

Stained glass has been used in the world's great cathedrals to glorify architecture and religion. Today old stained glass has become a favorite for collectors to use in the home. Many of the most striking contemporary designs have been inspired by Victorian glass.

Beveled glass refracts light and color as dramatically as a cut crystal wine goblet. A clear, fan-shaped panel by Bryer-Frank Studios (above) captures a whole palette of color from nearby objects.

Glowing sunlight illuminates recycled stained-glass panels, part of a collection belonging to Mike Hynes (right). Framed to flank one of the upright supports of the house, the panels become an unusual "headboard." The idea developed as architect Harry H. Gesner and designers Marjorie Bedell and Larry Laughlin worked to find a pleasing formula for furnishing a home where architectural elements dominate.

stained glass for the novice

As beautiful and complex as leaded and stained glass may seem, almost anyone can tackle an at-home project in this material. It is not an impossible accomplishment for the novice. Here is a simple way to reproduce one motif, then duplicate it two, three, or four times. The result is a color-splashed panel designed to enhance a window or clerestory.

By using one basic design element in stained and leaded glass, artist Brad Lewis develops a versatile project for beginners. The theme is based on a stylized California poppy design which can be used alone or duplicated to form four motifs for a wreath-shaped composition.

The basic design is drawn on a 16 by 16-inch square of white wrapping paper. Colors are roughed in, then three kinds of glass are chosen to establish various tones and translucencies. If four panels are assembled, as shown, the result is dramatic. It's a simple project, but as with any craft, it's wise to set aside a workspace that won't be disturbed. For instructions on making a stained-glass panel, turn the page.

1 gold	4 navy	7 green
2 violet	5 red	8 turquoise
3 orange	6 yellow	9 pink

making a stained-glass panel

Using Brad Lewis's poppy design, a stained-glass window can be reproduced in a home workshop. When enlarging the design, it's important to use heavy outlines that can be seen through the colored glass.

The numbers on the diagram indicate the suggested colors; use the chart below the diagram as the key. You may prefer, however, to make up your own color scheme.

All tools and materials are available at stained-glass supply stores as are various types of glass. For those who prefer in-person instructions, classes are conducted at schools, craft stores, and many stained-glass galleries.

TOOLS AND MATERIALS
For design:
a square ruler
white or graph paper
medium-tip marking pen
tracing pencils
colored marking pen

For cutting and wrapping glass:
cutting oil
cutter with ball end
small-wheeled cutter
breaking pliers
grozing pliers
grozing stone
copper foil
fid
farrier nails and hammer

1

For assembling and finishing:
wood strips for framing
50-50 solder
80-watt soldering iron
paste flux
oleic acid flux
patina
sponge and brush for clean-up
½-inch-wide zinc came for joining panels

1   Make a drawing 16 by 16 inches square. Use a medium tip dark marker to ensure easy visibility of each section of the design.

2   Fill in the drawing with colored pencils or markers to correspond with the glass colors that have been selected.

3   First, a note about the glass: antique glass is the predominant type used in this design. Opalescent glass is used for the border and the pink bud. Cathedral glass is used for the red poppy bud.

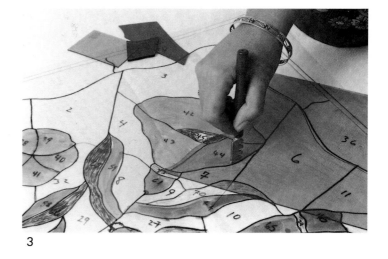

3

Place the appropriate piece of glass on top of the illustration. Dip a glass cutter into cutting oil. Holding cutter perpendicular to the glass, firmly scribe the glass to match the area in the drawing. Use *one continuous cutting motion* and do not retrace. For anyone who has never tried it before, it is a good idea to practice on scrap glass. Dark or opalescent glass may require the use of a strong backlight to facilitate visibility when cutting.

Grasp the glass firmly on one side with breaking pliers and on the other side with your free hand. Using even pressure, gradually press down and split glass apart.

If glass resists, tap it beneath the scribe mark from the underside with the ball end of the glass cutter. Use a smooth tapping motion. Curved cuts are most difficult to execute and will almost always require tapping.

At this point, it is necessary to smooth away any excess glass left on unclean cuts. To do so, nibble at chips with grozing pliers and lightly sand edges with a grozing stone.

4

As pieces are cut assemble them as they will appear in the finished panel. This procedure will help you visualize how the design is taking shape.

4   Mold ¼-inch adhesive copper foil around the edge of each piece of glass. Smooth down all sharp edges of the copper foil with the fid.

5   Place the colored drawing on a 20 by 20-inch board. Use two 16-inch wood strips to form a right angle. This frames the glass and holds it in place. Assemble the design in puzzle fashion.

To hold pieces together tightly, place flat-sided farrier nails at edge of each added section of glass. Remove and replace them as you build the design. After all pieces are secured in place, the window is ready to be completed.

Paint oleic acid over all exposed copper foil edging and use a soldering iron to melt 50-50 solder over the copper foil.

Then clean the window with a strong solution of detergent. Rinse well. To achieve the aged look of this completed window, apply patina overall. Lewis used ½-inch-wide zinc came strips to join the modules.

5

the grand statement

Every so often, a homeowner becomes a patron of the arts—not by collecting and displaying paintings or sculpture, but by commissioning a major work of art for the home. Such an event occurred when client, designer, and artisans had a sympathetic meeting of minds; this dramatic window was the result.

Designer Eszter Haraszty Colen is in love with nature in all its manifestations. It isn't often that such an artist has the opportunity to develop a total design concept for a client's house. But that chance came—and this spectacular window was but one of the ways artist and client shaped ideas for "living." Inspired by the wild and wonderful California poppy, this exacting work was planned by Haraszty, then executed by Judson Studios, where third-generation glaziers produce windows for churches, homes, and offices.

Although this flower-splashed window can be seen from the garden, its brilliance turns inward. It is art for private enjoyment and illustrates the way individuals are able to come together in the creation of small miracles for that very private place we call home.

211

photographers
and coordinators

The author wishes to thank Susan A. Grode, Aki Toyooka, Gregory Sokolowski, and Wai-Mei Fang.

Note: the home pictured on pages 10 and 13 was designed by architect Morton Hoppenfeld.